HOA WARRIOR II

The Game Changer for Winning HOA Disputes with AI Support

(AI-powered responses, letters, appeals, and timelines with step-by-step guidance for homeowners and trustees to tackle HOA issues)

by Shelly Marshall, Owner/Advocate
with contributions from Grok, an AI by xAI

If you live in an HOA, remember you don't actually own your own home. It's owned jointly by every member of the neighborhood. That means when your HOA gets sued the damage judgments are shared equally by every member of the neighborhood. If your board does something outrageous enough to precipitate a lawsuit you could face an outrageous special assessment to pay the damage award. ~Posted on April 1, 2015 by Ward Lucas

HOAWARRIOR.com

Second Edition 2025
Published by Day-By-Day.org

HOA WARRIOR: 20 Tactics for Fighting your HOA, all the way to court if necessary
ISBN 978-1-934569-10-8 Kindle Version
ISBN 978-1-934569-33-7 ePub Version
ISBN 978-1-934569-34-4 PDF & Print Version

HOA WARRIOR II: The Game Changer for Winning HOA Disputes with AI Support
ISBN 978-1-934569-71-9 Kindle Version
ISBN 978-1-934569-70-2 ePub Version
ISBN 978-1-934569-69-6 PDF & Print Version

TABLE OF CONTENTS

NOTE FROM THE AUTHOR

Welcome to the second edition of HOA Warrior II, your guide to winning disputes in Planned Development Communities (PDC)s, like HOAs, COAs, and POAs. It expands on the battle tactics in our first book, *HOA Warrior: Battle Tactics for Fighting your HOA, all the way to court if necessary*, to arm you with AI-powered tools. Whether you're a homeowner fighting a violation or a Trustee pushing for fairer board decisions, these strategies counter a vendor-driven industry, as critics like George Staropoli argue about organizations like the Community Association Institute (CAI), which seems to prioritize vendor interests over homeowners. But as a trade organization, that is to be expected; they take care of their paying members which are the vendors for the HOAs.

I'm Shelly Marshall, a homeowner advocate who battled rogue boards in Grass Valley, Utah. A director's outburst—"Shut up, we don't have to run every little thing by you people!"—ignited my mission to help you reclaim your homeowner rights. I don't want you to suffer like Tom and Anita Radcliff, who lost their $300,000 home over a $120 HOA debt forgotten during Tom's illness. They regained their home through legal action, but at great financial and emotional cost. That's the kind of injustice we're fighting to prevent. The first edition's templates were hard to adapt to everyone's unique HOA rules. Now, with contributions from Grok, an AI by xAI, this book provides step-by-step guidance to craft tailored responses, letters, appeals, and timelines for disputes over pets, paint, parking, solar panels, or drought-resistant landscaping—all in plain, neighborly language, not legalese. Whether disputing a fine or advocating for fair policies as a trustee, these AI tools save time, money, and stress. Want to shape your HOA's future? Consider running for your board. Visit hoawarrior.com for AI prompt libraries and advocacy updates, or share your story at info@hoawarrior.com. Let's make your home your castle again.

DISCLAIMER

Shelly Marshall and Grok, an AI by xAI, are not attorneys, licensed real estate agents, or certified managers. Our suggestions, based on Shelly's experience as a homeowner advocate and PDC member, are not professional legal advice. This book provides informational guidance only. You must research your state's laws, as PDC regulations vary by state and judicial interpretations differ. Even if we cite federal, state, or local laws, our interpretations may not be correct. For serious issues like foreclosures or lawsuits, consult an attorney, paralegal, or legal firm. Verify AI-generated content against official sources (e.g., leg.state.fl.us for Florida, davis-stirling.com for California and so on).

> **Factoid** *There were 10,000 association-governed communities in the United States in 1970, and by 2025, the number had reached 370,000 to 390,000 (depending on your source) with 12 new associations forming every day according to iPropertyManagement, in their article: HOA Statistics. More than half of all homeowners live in PDCs.*

FOREWORD

The imposition of forced membership residential associations on American homeowners is fraught with misinformation, misunderstandings, and miscommunication. New homeowners are surprised to find themselves subject to restrictions and expenses they were not aware of when they bought their "home". But the nasty surprises of the powers conferred on the paid and unpaid managers/leaders of the development are never ending.

Shelly Marshall demystifies many of the sources of confusion for both the homeowner and the board member who steps up to fill the role. In a folksy and conversational manner she writes an easy to read and understand booklet explaining the different types of associations, where and how they derive their powers and how to protect your assets. A subject that could be excruciatingly dry and dull, is brought to life with stories from around the country highlighting the points she is making. She connects the dots, explains where to look for information and reminds the homeowner of probably the most important piece of advice: **Do Your Homework.** This is very important because, as Shelly points out, not only are all governing documents unique to the individual association but state statutes vary dramatically and the governing parameters vary with the type of association, (HOA, POA, Condo).

Shelly also tells us that we are our own best advocates. That means we have to know what we are talking about and above all, to be professional. Very sound advice.

She addresses board members as well and reminds them they need not always be on the defensive or try to hide information from their fellow owners because they are unsure of what they are doing. The association is supposed to be a "community" where everyone is a member.

The book is full of practical recommendations for every day life and includes sample forms the reader can use whether as a homeowner or as a board member trying to manage the association. A must have for quick reference and as an aid to understanding what we have bought.

[*Author's Note: For this second edition, sample forms have been replaced with AI-powered prompts to craft tailored responses, letters, appeals, and timelines, making it easier to tackle HOA disputes with confidence.*]

Shu Bartholomew
Host of On the Commons
http://onthecommons.us/
News and Views about Homeowner Associations

INTRODUCTION

It is recommended that you thoroughly understand the influence of the vendors!

Running a Planned Development Community (PDC) like an HOA, COA, or POA requires discipline, transparency, and organization. Poorly run boards falter, with volunteer Trustees issuing inconsistent fines, sloppy warning letters, or unrecorded decisions, often ignoring state codes or governing documents. This chaos fuels disputes over pets, paint, parking, solar panels, or drought-resistant landscaping, leaving Members frustrated and powerless. Clear, unbiased policies are essential to align everyone. Yet, PDCs begin with developer-drafted documents, sidelining Member input. As lots sell, challenges arise: elections shift boards, boards hire management companies, and companies involve attorneys, each with distinct priorities. In my view, some management companies and attorneys, often affiliated with trade organizations like the Community Association Institute, may guide boards toward policies that emphasize vendor interests over Member needs, as critics like George Staropoli note. This book empowers Members with AI tools to fight for fairness.

For this second edition, we've replaced complicated templates with AI-powered prompts so that you can produce well-written responses, letters, appeals, and timelines. This empowers homeowners and trustees to tackle disputes with confidence.

> **Factoid:** *As a top consultant and past HOA manager, Vicki MacHale warns, "Did you know the **#1** request Realtors receive is to see homes outside of an HOA? {...} I think back to how many times I've been involved with discussions where industry leaders sat around and pointed fingers at "crazy" homeowners, board members, competitors, and legislators for the continued degradation of our industry. How they laughed when they proudly proclaimed, "I would NEVER live in a Homeowners Association."* ~ IndependentAmericanCommunities.com

What does this mean for Members?

In a well-run PDC, you'll need precise, law-cited responses referencing your CC&Rs or state statutes to address issues. In a chaotic PDC, AI-powered prompts can make boards back off by demonstrating that you know as much—or more—than they do. Consider Horace, a Grass Valley, Utah, resident who frustrated all the authorities. He lived in a 5th wheel with his family and 75 dogs, claiming he was "camping," not residing. He built a partial structure, calling it an "art studio" just under the square footage requiring a county permit. No camping time limit existed in county ordinances, so no one could stop him from living in the fifth wheel and building a structure beside it that he used as a living room. Our CC&Rs allowed unrestricted animals, overriding county ordinances, so his vicious dogs were untouchable. Acting as his own attorney, Horace exploited every loophole, filing complaints and lawsuits that intimidated the board and county, exhausting everyone and so, in the end, they left him alone. I don't suggest mimicking Horace's antics so that your board or county leave you alone. We, Grok and I, are going to demonstrate how you can leverage your position by using AI to help level the playing field. You can learn how to use AI-powered prompts to craft fact-backed, law-cited responses that deter boards from challenging you.

Here's another example. Our Grass Valley attorney, who specialized in association law, supported board decisions I found questionable. When homeowners requested records they were legally entitled to, the board asked the attorney to draft a restrictive policy that I believed conflicted with Utah's Corporate Code. I wrote a response letter to the policy he drafted, citing the law, and stopped the policy. However, it took me *days* to research the Utah Code and County Ordinances, until I found what I needed. If I had had Grok in those days, it would have been a few minutes to do the *same amount of work*. People don't usually have days to do this work or unlimited funds to hire an attorney to do the work, when confronting HOA nonsense.

So members give up and issues go unaddressed. The board and management get away with questionable, and often unreasonable, actions that thwart common sense. As the saying goes, "You can't fight City Hall"—until now. AI is a game changer, fundamentally shifting the dynamics of Planned Development Communities and vendor trade organizations often rendering Members nearly powerless, leaving them to foot the bills while sidelining their voices. With HOA Warrior II, AI empowers Members to respond swiftly and effectively, leveling the playing field in minutes, not months, so they're no longer left holding the bag.

Director or Trustee?

HOW CAN HOA WARRIOR II HELP A BOARD?

Your board members are neighbors—some are caring and organized, carrying out duties rationally and equitably. Others turn into power-hungry "dictocrats," enforcing the three petty P's of every Association: Pets, Paint, and Parking, so petty as to defy reason. Often they are retired folk with too much time on their hands. These little dictocrats impose their version of utopia on association members forgetting that you are a community and their friends and neighbors, not their serfs.

> **Factoid:** *One northern California couple, Tom and Anita Radcliff, lost their $300,000 home over an unpaid $120 HOA debt. After foreclosing, the association sent a three-day notice to vacate. They auctioned the home for $70,000. Tom was ill, and Anita forgot the bill; no one contacted them until foreclosure. They eventually regained it through legal action, but at great cost. ~Benson, Sara E.; DeBat, Don (2014). Escaping Condo Jail*

As volunteer directors, board members need guidance to fulfill their duties effectively—perhaps that's you. Association trade organizations, such as the Community Association Institute (CAI), offer board training, but critics, like those cited at the end of this introduction, argue it may encourage reliance on vendor 'experts' who profit from board contracts, potentially prioritizing vendor interests over homeowners. This perceived conflict, where trade groups train boards that hire their affiliated vendors, underscores the need for transparency in board decisions.

> **Factoid**: *Homeowners Associations ("HOAs") are, essentially, a "private" government—an organization that has the legal authority to tax. In the HOA world, we call this tax either "dues" or an "assessment" ("dues" is the term used most commonly, but "assessment" is actually the correct term). ~Chuck Fowler March 28, 2014 Colorado*

The deck is unfortunately stacked against the owner who finances this whole debacle. Little did we know that becoming Members of planned communities meant that our property rights and even our privacy rights were signed away. We thought life in a Planned Development Community would be better and our liabilities fewer; that is what we were told by developers, real estate agents, and of course the CAI. By the time homeowners learn that they signed away their rights and incurred potentially *much more* liability, it is too late. They are there and often stuck. Here is an email I received as I was preparing this book from a man who came to the United States because he thought he would have more freedom. (I left his broken English intact so as to accentuate his recent position in coming to America and finding he is less free than in Vietnam!)

> *Hello Shelly,*
>
> *I'm fight abusive HOA and found your web site, bought your book HOA Warrior. In the book, I love your statement "outlaw all HOA", so I have this email to you. I risked my life in escaping abusive power Vietnamese Communist 2 decades ago as a Vietnamese Boat People, almost got killed by Thai pirate. Now I'm experiencing abusive power by HOA!!!*
>
> *I could not believe HOA business is allowed in the most civilized country whose outstanding constitution against abusing power by even allowing people to arm themselves to fight back whoever abusing power to harm their lives, by creating 3 branches of government to balance power.*

To me, HOA business is violating the constitution because:

1) *It violates the basic right to live freely without hassle*
2) *It abuses power in creating their own rules and dictates people to follow like a law*

There is a key difference between laws and rules. Based on the constitution, laws are made by the congress and approved by the president. Law breakers must be assumed innocent until judged by a very strict judiciary procedure. While rules are simply made within an organization, like school or workplace (company, association,). Rule breakers are suspended or expelled from organization or fired from workplace. People follow rules as they get benefit from the organization making those rules, say employee paycheck. Why do I have to follow your rules when I get no benefit from HOA, but hassle? On contrary, HOA get benefit from me via HOA fee, it just makes no sense at all to me. If the HOA found I broke the rule, all they could do is to expel me from the HOA.

I could not believe HOA is allowed to dictate people how to behave in their personal life similar to attacking private life, contradict to privacy law! There's no difference between house WITH and WITHOUT HOA, besides HOA hassle like ridiculous rules and fee (10% of monthly mortgage), .

I wish to coordinate with ALL homeowners to outlaw all HOA for the better life in the most civilized country like USA. I'm thinking to create a web site "outlaw-HOA.org" for this purpose.

Sincerely, ~Duy-Ky

So Duy-Ky discovered like most of us do, *after it is too late*, that HOA land in America is far from free or protected! But starting a website, although good, is just not working--at least not fast enough. CIC Members are organizing, we are advocating and we are finding attorneys who will actually help the homeowner. A long hard battle awaits us.

In the meantime, how do you protect yourself? That is what our new secret weapon is all about, putting your best and most professional foot forward, taking the bully by the horns, and protecting yourself as best you can, without costing you your retirement, reputation, or home.

PROTECT YOURSELF INFO.

The Community Association Institute (CAI), present in most states, claims to represent vendors, boards, and homeowners. Critics, like George Staropoli in 'Is CAI a Coercive HOA Monopoly?' and Jan Bergemann in a February 9, 2004, opinion piece, argue its paying membership—mostly attorneys, management companies, and contractors—prioritizes vendor interests, often supporting legislation that may favor vendors over homeowners. While CAI provides some useful resources, I believe it encourages boards to rely on profit-driven vendors, potentially at homeowners' expense. For more, explore Staropoli's article (pvtgov.info) or Bergemann's documented critique (ccfj.net/).

CHAPTER ONE: THE FOUNDATION OF YOUR RESPONSE TO ANY HOA ISSUE

Critics of Planned Development Communities (PDCs) say a small group of homeowners can't possibly stand up to the power of HOA boards, professional management companies, and CAI-affiliated attorneys. That's why you must protect yourself as soon as you notice things going awry.

> ***Factoid:*** *From Star Trek, the Borg are a collection of species that have been turned into cybernetic organisms functioning as drones in a hive mind called the Collective, or the Hive (see above cartoon). The Borg use a process called assimilation to force other species into the Collective. The Borg's ultimate goal is "achieving perfection."*

YOU, AND YOUR AI, ARE YOUR OWN BEST ADVOCATES

Lawyers are too expensive and lack the time to review all your documents—CC&Rs, bylaws, or pages of laws on corporations, contracts, real estate, consumer protection, disabilities, and federal codes. You may not have time either, but when trapped in an HOA dispute, you must bite the bullet and become your own expert. Many newcomers to HOA horrors assume there's a regulatory agency to help. A few states have them, like ombudsmen or investigators, but they're often backlogged for months and have limited power. But our AI assistant does have the time and the power to do some of this work. So our secret weapon will help you (us) fight back. Before we get into those specifics, you need to thoroughly understand what you are up against in order to understand the best prompts for using your AI.

Take Colorado's HOA Information Office and Resource Center (IORC). These concerned citizens investigated the increasing problems arising with HOAs and published this:

> *The IORC's 2011 report lists these problems as "the failure to follow corporate governance rules and procedures of the HOA; the transparency of the board directors, particularly as it related to the finances of the HOA; and harassment and bullying of homeowners by the board of directors and management company by arbitrary fining, preclusion from providing input into the associations' affairs, and verbal harassment. These complaint types ... substantially interfered with a homeowner's ability to enjoy his property and to have avenues of democratic participation in the HOA to remedy their issues."*

This captures the homeowners' struggle in a nutshell, doesn't it? The irony is, you get to pay for the harassment, bullying, unfairness, lack of transparency, lawsuits that arise, and so on via your assessments. Your assessments fund the entire industry.

WE ARE DOING THIS FOR YOUR OWN GOOD

Trade organizations like the Community Association Institute (CAI) and their political action committees, along with some legislators, claim their laws protect homeowners—but do they? As a former CAI member in Utah, where I briefly served on their legislative review committee, I witnessed attorneys drafting bills like the Utah Community Association Act (57-8a, 2004, amended regularly). I challenged provisions that, despite 'protective' claims, allowed boards to incorporate without member notification or consent if the declaration permits, as per Utah Code § 57-8a-228. When I questioned a lead author about this practice, which I found troubling, he sidestepped the issue. Imagine waking up to find your unincorporated community is now a corporation, without your input! Such secretive incorporation can lead to Articles of Incorporation that limit homeowner rights, shifting decision-making power—over elections, budgets, contracts, or rules—away from you, the homeowner.

I pressed a bill author about boards making major decisions without owner input, citing our Grass Valley board's secretive incorporation that altered voting rights in the Articles of Incorporation. He dismissed my concerns, claiming, 'Boards are generally good; they wouldn't take advantage.' I found this response overly optimistic. Utah's Community Association Act (57-8a-215) grants boards broad budget-making power, requiring 51% of all members—not just a quorum—to reject a budget. In Grass Valley, with 80% absentee owners, we rarely see 20% attendance at annual meetings, making it nearly impossible to block problematic budgets. Additionally, Utah Code § 57-8a-303 allows non-judicial foreclosure, enabling boards to seize homes without court oversight. In Grass Valley, poor bookkeeping led to some homeowners facing a CAI-affiliated collections attorney, incurring high fees and risking their homes without judicial review. These experiences lead many advocates, myself included, to question CAI's 'protective' claims, viewing their influence skeptically.

FOXES GUARDING THE HEN HOUSE

To stand up to the mighty trade organization foxes guarding your hen house, you must be prepared and professional. Being prepared means familiarizing yourself in the areas listed below, especially when they pertain to your situation. Being professional means presenting yourself well, using the guidelines and strategies in this book to tackle disputes with confidence.

These are the topics you must familiarize yourself with:

a) County Plat Maps
b) Deed Restrictions (CC&Rs)
c) Articles of Incorporation
d) Bylaws
e) County Zoning Laws
f) Rules and Regulations of your association
g) Applicable State Codes
   1) Corporate Law
   2) Contract Law
   3) Consumer Protection Law
   4) Disability Law
   5) Discrimination Law
   6) Environmental Law

Trying to research these numerous topics, was once a nightmare, taking hours, days, or weeks. Members disputing a violation, contesting a "late" payment that wasn't late, or seeking a variance for architectural styles often gave up due to the time and cost. I know—I spent three years fighting our HOA, losing countless hours. Most homeowners don't have that time, money, or experience. If you can't or won't research your documents and state codes, you may face fines or worse. No agency will swoop in to save you.

Enter our secret weapon: Artificial Intelligence. AI does what you can't—researching and crafting responses in minutes. This book shows you how to choose the best AI, create effective prompts, and generate accurate responses, letters, appeals, and timelines tailored to your state and HOA issues. Now, many more homeowners can confront errant boards with confidence.

Fighting a board of trustees takes time and effort you may not want to devote to it. Take me, for example; I know *way more than I ever wanted to* about corporate law, association law, the Constitution, federal law, the CAI, and how the state legislators work. I won many battles, lost a few, and now live outside the HOA system, for obvious reasons. AI could have saved me those three years of struggle, both financially and timewise (time taken from my business and family)—had it been available.

AI isn't a cure-all for HOA woes, but it levels the playing field. It researches in minutes what took me weeks of grueling effort. Boards supported by organizations like the CAI wield significant influence through vendor resources and legislative advocacy, but AI gives you a fighting chance.

HRE 1 You can uncover loopholes like Horace did to stop board harassment, but do it respectfully and professionally, avoiding lawsuits like the slander or ultra vires claims I faced from board actions. In minutes, not months, you can protect your rights without losing your life to the fight. AI even aids in court, slashing legal research costs for escalating HOA disputes. You, my friend, are in a far better position than I was when my warrior days began.

> **Factoid**: *Owners who speak out about suspected fraud are often slapped with Nuisance lawsuits for slander. Slander nuisance lawsuits are so prevalent that 26 states have enacted statutory protections against Strategic Lawsuit Against Public Participation (SLAPP). SLAPP lawsuits attempt to censor, intimidate, and silence critics who cannot afford to mount or sustain a defense. Anti-SLAPP laws are designed to protect individuals and corporations who are sued for exercising their First Amendment rights of free speech and petition.* ~Benson, Sara E.; DeBat, Don (2014-11-05). Escaping Condo Jail (Kindle Locations 305-316). Kindle Edition

AI CAN SUMMARIZE THE LAW & DOCUMENTS YOU NEED TO BEGIN

Facing an HOA dispute can feel like climbing a mountain of legal documents and state codes. Your secret weapon, AI, changes that. In minutes, it summarizes your CC&Rs, bylaws, Articles of Incorporation, county zoning laws, and state codes—corporate, contract, consumer protection, disability, discrimination, or environmental—tailored to your issue, like a pet restriction or solar panel denial. You don't need weeks or a law degree; AI empowers you to understand your rights and respond professionally.

Exactly how to find and use AI is covered in Chapter Three, with prompts and examples in Chapter Three and Chapter Nine. First, you need to understand the basis for standing up to a board, law firm, or management company, which explains the reasons behind AI prompts and their limitations and cautions. The rights and duties of home, property, or condo owners are governed partly by statutory law and partly by the "contract" between you and your association, found in the Protective Covenants (your CC&Rs), and other governing documents. But often, there are contradictions between all these documents and laws. One law says one thing while another law contradicts the first law. Or likewise, your plat map may say something that conflicts with state law or your bylaws. In these instances, the higher body of law and documents supersedes the lower one.

Here is an interesting dilemma relative to Utah State Code.

> If the governing documents of an Association allowed a Board to charge interest *and* a late fee for past-due assessments, that may be overturned in a court of law because the Utah Corporate Code does not allow both interest *and* late fees to be charged to members, only one *or* the other (§16-4-301-1-a).
> However, in a*ssociation law* for Utah, Associations may charge both interest and late fees, if allowed in the Declaration (§57-8a-301).
>
> So, if an incorporated HOA's CC&Rs allow both interest and late fees, but the corporate code prohibits both. Which governs? Since the corporate code was enacted long before HOA code, you'd expect it to prevail. Most likely, a court would decide, possibly ruling that corporate law trumps or viewing the CC&Rs as a contract superseding corporate law—who knows?

In any case, here is the hierarchy you are looking for:

The Hierarchy of the Law

1. Federal Statute
2. State Code
3. County Ordinances

Hierarchy of Governing Documents

1. Plat Map
2. Protective Covenants
3. Articles of Incorporation
4. Bylaws
5. Rules and Regulations

PICKING YOUR BATTLES

When your HOA board demands money or compliance—say, a fine for a late fee, overweight pet, or wrong paint color—and you disagree, you must educate yourself on all sides of the issue. Start with the rules. Ask yourself: Did I really break a rule or regulation?

1. Did I break a rule or regulation?

___**No**. If you didn't break a rule, follow your association's dispute or redress procedures. Using Chapter Nine, find the right category, have your AI assistant research the issue, compare it to your governing documents **(exact prompts are in the Chapter Three)**, and prepare a response explaining why you didn't violate the rule or why it doesn't apply (your AI can do most of this). Deliver it as your HOA requires—AI will confirm if a registered letter or signed receipt from the manager or a board member is best. Then, hope your board is reasonable, not vindictive.

___**Yes.** If you did break a rule—maybe you missed it or a guest caused the violation—you're responsible. Pay the fine, correct the issue, and move on.

Factoid: *Boards have limited power to change documents, rules, or policies. Most covenants and corporate laws require a homeowner majority to approve bylaw changes. Yet, many boards sidestep this by altering house rules, which are as binding as bylaws but often don't need homeowner approval. "Even if you were given the rules today, they're probably already outdated because [boards] constantly change rules at whim," says Elizabeth McMahon, co-founder of the American Homeowners Resource Center, a San Juan Capistrano, California, consumer group. ~American Homeowners Resource Center*

2. Even with an AI assistant, don't dispute any sanctions unless:

a) **The rule is selectively enforced,** and you believe you're targeted for some reason. Decide if it's worth disputing on this basis, hoping the board is reasonable, or if complying saves the hassle of a fight. "Selective enforcement" means a board can't enforce a rule against one owner while ignoring the same violation by another. AI will find the correct citation, as most documents and state laws prohibit arbitrary or capricious enforcement. But boards can often do what they want, and short of suing, you have little recourse.

Example: A Colorado couple renting in an HOA, with kids parking cars in front of their unit and on rocks, got a violation notice. They were upset because other residents' similar violations were ignored. Colorado's selective enforcement statute offers some protection, but they face an uphill battle. Judges often rule that a violation stands unless you prove others weren't cited—photos alone aren't enough. If you suspect targeting (e.g., for being Hispanic), you still must prove it. (reference "d" below: The rule is discriminatory)

Factoid: *Montana is one of the few states with clear selective enforcement laws. Enacted in 2025, Mont. Code Ann. § 70-17-210 requires a covenant to be "equally and consistently enforced" across all properties for at least two years for an HOA to enforce it. This means an HOA cannot selectively fine one homeowner (e.g., for a violation ignored in others) unless it has consistently applied the covenant for two years, strengthening your defense. ~Mont. House Bill 147 (2025)*

b) **It is not a real rule**—not in the documents or not properly voted in by the board or members, per your governing documents. Decide if it's worth pointing out the rule's absence or is it easier to pay a $100 fine. With your AI assistant, you can quickly confirm the rules existence and ask the board to drop the fine until the rule is documented. Pay any fine, even if unjustified, by the due date to avoid extra penalties during an appeal. Seek reimbursement later if you prevail.

Example: At Virginia's Reston Homeowners Association, only residents using pools and tennis courts paid for upkeep. In 1990, the board polled members to make everyone pay, but over 70% opposed it. The board pushed it through anyway, raising fees 26%. "They disregarded the will of the people," says Thierry Gaudin, a Reston homeowner, "and that was wrong." Associations generally require members to approve new rules not in the covenants, so the members may have successfully fought this, but that entails courts and high legal fees. ~Cyber Citizens for Justice, Inc.

c) **The rule is contradicted** by a higher document or law. Your AI assistant can cite the discrepancy in your documents or state code and prepare an appeal based on the conflicting rule.

Example: Remember Horace from the Introduction? He kept 75 dogs! The association tried to enforce a county ordinance limiting residents to four dogs without a kennel license. But the CC&Rs allowed unrestricted animals, and in this subdivision, covenants superseded county ordinances. Neither the association nor county officials could stop Horace's dogs, as the county had approved the subdivision's covenants.

d) **The rule is discriminatory.** Under the Fair Housing Act (hud.gov/helping-americans/fair-housing-act-overview), certain activities targeting protected classes are unlawful:

1. Refuse to rent or sell housing
2. Refuse to negotiate for housing
3. Make housing unavailable
4. Set different terms, conditions, or privileges for sale or rental
5. Provide different housing services or facilities
6. Falsely deny that housing is available for inspection, sale or rental
7. For profit, persuade owners to sell or rent (blockbusting)
8. Deny any access to or membership in a facility or service (such as a multiple listing service) related to the sale of housing

9. Refuse to make reasonable accommodations in rules or services if necessary for a disabled person to use the housing
10. Refuse to allow a disabled person to make reasonable accommodations to his/her dwelling
11. Threaten or interfere with anyone making a fair housing complaint
12. Refuse to provide municipal services, property insurance or hazard insurance for dwellings, or providing such services or insurance differently

    Example 1: Federal and state laws prohibit HOAs from discriminating against families with children. An HOA rule banning bike riding or skateboarding is fine if it applies to everyone, not just kids. Recently, a mother in an HOA won a lawsuit against "Adult" swim time and "Adult Only" common areas, which a federal judge ruled violated the Fair Housing Act as discriminatory.

    Example 2: Some HOAs ban renting to registered sex offenders. This might seem discriminatory, but sex offenders aren't a protected class under federal or state law. So, an HOA may adopt such a restriction without violating state or federal laws. (hindmansanchez.com)

e) **The rule has been ignored for years,** then suddenly enforced. Like selective enforcement, rules or deed restrictions ignored for a period can be deemed "waived," losing enforceability across the community. Each state's waiver laws vary—some as short as 90 days, others up to four years.

> **Example:** A Florida homeowner, seeing neighbors with pets despite a no-pet rule, got a Chihuahua. After five years, a new board decided to enforce the rule. Under Florida's four-year waiver law, his pet was grandfathered in. But if the board notifies all owners that the rule will be enforced going forward, past pets stay get to stay, while new ones are banned, renewing the rule's enforceability.

Have your AI assistant review and analyze the applicable laws and documents before starting your battle. First, understand all relevant documents and state codes to confirm if they support the board's view or yours. If the documents clearly back the board, I strongly advise complying.

The main exception to complying is if you suspect the board or documents violate state or federal law. Your AI should uncover this with the right prompts, covered in Chapters Three thorough Nine. For example, an HOA's mailbox rules can't contradict USPS standards (e.g., forbidding decorations is fine, but not placement or height interfering with delivery). Or, under the FCC's 1996 Act, boards can't ban satellite dishes. Knowing these laws, which AI can summarize, makes a huge difference in your fight.

IN CONCLUSION

I hope most of your needs won't involve fighting infractions, violations, or your board. Instead, I'd love to see you seeking architectural approvals, permission to plant flowers, or petitions for a second pet. Conversely, I urge boards not to use AI assistants to harass members but to ensure business is legal, transparent, and fair.

I want you, the homeowner, to look professional when approaching your board for anything. That's why I'm adamant about understanding your documents and relevant laws. These strategies give you a professional edge, but only if you do the preparatory work to build a solid foundation. Know what you're talking about and don't rely solely on AI—*trust but verify*!

I want Trustees reading this to act professionally and carry out duties fairly and authoritatively. Do this by following rules, not making them up, willy-nilly. Use your AI assistant to run elections and confirm compliance with your documents before enforcing rules and making life hard on your members. Don't respond exclusively to the retired "squeaky wheels" who constantly spy on their neighbors. Resist becoming that retired squeaky wheel yourself. Remember, those you target today could be on tomorrow's board. Ask yourself, "How do I want to be treated?"

In Grass Valley, once my friends were elected to the board, the new president acquired all the emails from the POA attorney that pertained to our Association. It was eye-opening. One Member who was not actually on the board, was running the show from the shadows--telling the president and vice president what to say. This Member directed the Grass Valley attorney to do his bidding and write letters to Members to shut them up. There were numerous letters and resolutions created at the direction of this puppet-master and no one realized he was in charge, not our board. One letter which was meant for me, I didn't receive. Not sure why. But the many thousands of dollars wasted trying to "control" us was criminal. And, ironically, there I sat as a new board member, reading all this garbage. Be careful when on the board. You must keep in mind that next week this Member you consider to be a pest, may be sitting where you are.

Our AI examples are generic, not state-specific. Grok and I will guide you in using prompts, with examples of AI-prepared documents for members to boards and boards to members, in Chapter Three through Nine. They cover basic HOA needs but aren't exhaustive. Some communities have 50+ forms, from "Application for Tree Trimming" to "Waiver for Using a Barbecue Grill." This book isn't that complex. Instead, Grok and I aim to save you time, money, and stress with guidelines to prompt your AI and verify its outputs. Chapter Two, is a sort of "white paper" for boards, helping new trustees avoid mistakes and heartache by applying its principles. Your turn to serve as a Trustees will arise and I hope you rise to the occasion.

CHAPTER TWO: From Neighbor to Trustee: Let AI Protect Your Association from YOU, When Elected to the Board

As well as empowering members to protect themselves, I want you, the board member, to safeguard the association. When elected to a board, volunteers often face subtle power dynamics they don't fully notice, and their *mindset* shifts. In our Grass Valley, Utah, association, we replaced problematic boards, only to see new ones repeat the same behaviors we fought against. It's a sneaky change—board members don't see it in themselves. I once believed the CAI 'groomed' boards to favor vendors, as critics like George Staropoli suggest, but I've come to see this trade organization as capitalizing on the natural tendencies of board members who gain power and then misuse it.

> **Factoid:** *Research shows nonprofit board members, including HOA trustees, often change after elections, adopting aggressive or bullying behaviors to assert control. The shift stems from a "leadership" mindset, assuming their role grants superior authority. Some enforce strict rules on members while excusing their own noncompliance, believing their role justifies exceptions, saying "somebody has to do it." ~Didericksen, J., et al. (2024), Administrative Sciences, Mollard Consulting (2024)*

This mindset sneaks up on you. A member requests a copy of expenditures or a contact list, and you think, "What do they want? Are they accusing me of stealing? It's not their business!" or "They can't have that—our attorney says there's privacy issues!" You rationalize withholding information members are legally entitled to. You might not consider that this neighbor could be on next year's board or that all owners, as business partners, have rights to association records under most state corporate codes. Don't let power cloud your judgment.

Questions aren't attacks. As a trustee, it's your duty to keep members informed about the association's business. Don't create a little fiefdom, going defensive or launching counterattacks at every request. Sigh. Be transparent, not territorial.

Factoid: *Contributing to a research paper, Shelly Marshall (your author) has found that "there are differential power roles in a condominium" once owners are on the board. They become more defensive and condescending toward their neighbors' opinions and participation in the affairs of the association. It is a common behavioral response to power and must be actively counteracted so as not to taint the community. Marshall, M. J., Marshall, S., & Goonan, D. (2018). HOA power relationship, Housing and Society, 45(3), 186–205.*

In our Grass Valley, Utah, association, after replacing an unresponsive board with member-friendly Trustees, they created a handbook outlining Trustee and Member duties. It included guidelines for running the association. But the next board tossed it out and ignored prepared templates for ballots, tally sheets, proxies, and notices. Their non-compliant ballots, without adherence to state code, led to a challenged election costing our association thousands to redo. Pride isn't worth the price.

You don't need to redo your predecessors' documents and paperwork. Even if you replaced a trustee you disliked, their system—minutes, elections, notices—likely worked. Don't let pettiness stop you from using what's effective. If the prior board was incompetent, you may need to start fresh, but chances are some processes were fine. Use past board expertise and your AI assistant to analyze forms and records for accuracy. This can easily be done using the prompts we'll provide. Don't insult members by wasting time redoing what works—focus your energy on improving the HOA system.

CREATE FORMS, DOCUMENTS, & LETTERS USING YOUR AI ASSISTANT

You can build a complete library of forms, templates, guidelines, and a timeline of essential duties to keep your association on track. With your AI assistant's help, this collection will be well-rounded and tailored to your community's needs. If your association uses a management company, they likely provide forms already. Compare theirs to our guidelines and decide if updating some with language that reflects your community's spirit outshines their sterile versions.

Online sites sell association-specific documents, some excellent but costly when bought individually. For sensitive documents like lien or collection notices, trustees may prefer state-specific forms to ensure compliance with state code. Yet, with AI's speed and proper prompts, you can create these yourself, saving funds. If using a collection agency, they'll provide forms meeting industry standards, but you can request friendlier, more respectful wording. Use your good sense, always asking, "How would I want to be treated?"

Factoid: *Community associations can range in size from as small as two-unit associations to large-scale, master-planned communities with more than 30,000 units.*

YOU MAY ALREADY HAVE THE FORMS YOU NEED, LET AI IMPROVE THEM

If your association has been established for years and uses a management company, you likely have a library of forms already. But these may be overly complex, outdated, or worst of all, sterile and member-unfriendly. Aggressive, unsympathetic letters and notices make members defensive and angry. A few kind words and a touch of fairness can encourage compliance without frustration. For example, a ballot might say, "Ballots not in compliance with these instructions shall be rejected." Instead, try, "We regret that ballots not following this format cannot be counted, per state code." Which feels better?

Just a word or two can make a difference. Add "Please" before instructions and "Thank you" when requesting compliance. Members want to know you care. Review your letters, forms, and even outdoor signs, asking:

- How can I add a personal touch?
- How can I use "We" and "Us" instead of "Us" and "Them"?
- Can I say "Trustee" instead of "Director"?
- What wording feels friendly and respectful, not like legalese or superiority?

With "personal touch" prompts directed to your AI ally (thoroughly covered in Chapter Three), you can upload your documents to your AI assistant and ask them to enhance their tone and impact. A little thought can totally transform relationships and perceptions with your neighbors. You can choose legalese or neighborese to communicate with members. Here are a few examples:

Legalese or Neighborese

Legalese says "violation" while Neighborese says "noncompliance"

Legalese says "resident or occupant" while Neighborese says "partner or neighbor"

Legalese says "Director" while Neighborese says "Trustee"

Legalese says "Penalty" while Neighborese says "Enforcement fee"

Legalese says "warning" while Neighborese says "reminder"

Legalese capitalizes "Trustee" and not "member" while Neighborese capitalizes both

As a board member, never forget that you are a *partner* with your *neighbors* in the community.

You likely aren't reading this book if your association is trouble-free, so creating new member-friendly communications and forms can make more of difference than you realize. It could reset the whole atmosphere of your community. AI can provide owner-friendly documents using the right prompts (see Chapter Three through Nine), keeping them sympathetic and respectful, not harsh or obnoxious. Have your association attorney review critical documents, like notices or ballots, but don't let them rewrite them into harsh legalese, no matter their reasoning. You don't need to spend heavily on attorneys to design forms or draft every response to member inquiries. A quick attorney review of AI-generated documents ensures legal compliance while keeping communications in neighborese. Using AI saves your association money—it's far cheaper to review a document than create one.

Lawyers may advise you to enforce all documents with a firm hand

IN CONCLUSION

Vindictive boards create unhappy communities. Petty, senseless actions—like punishing so-called "rule-breakers" at neighbors' or lawyers' constant urging—hurt everyone. Management firms and vendors, often affiliated with CAI, may push harsh tactics, claiming it's to protect property values. In my opinion, such tactics, as seen in a now-removed webpage for a powerful HOA law firm stated, "*{owners} are forced to decide if they should make their car payment, mortgage payment, or homeowner assessment payment. With so many people facing financial strain, it is important that homeowner associations let their owners know their bill must be paid first and, if it is not, there will be serious consequences.*" They even promised "protected" account collections, where "the owner may not see their own account; only the association and manager has access!" Possibly removed due to exposure from advocates like me, this shows the attack-dog mentality.

> **Factoid:** *Research shows HOAs often use "abusive" collection tactics, like piling on thousands in fees and penalties, ignoring homeowner struggles. LS Carlson Law, defending homeowners, warns that unpaid dues can spiral fast into legal battles, violating fair debt collection laws. ~LS Carlson Law (2024),*

If you're reasonable enough to read this book (and read this far) and create owner-friendly forms, you're not as stubborn as many boards I've encountered. Resist pressure from trade organizations like Community Association Institute, National Association of Realtors, or Institute of Real Estate Management, which represent vendor interests, to adopt hard-line stances under 'duty and responsibility' rhetoric. Heavy-handed attitudes destroy communities, and you can—and should—refuse to fuel it.

Consider the 2008 feud in northern Virginia between Sam and Maria Farran and their HOA over a political sign four inches too large. The board, claiming it would lower property values, demanded removal. The Farrans cut the sign in half, planting both halves in their yard, angering and embarrassing the board. The board retaliated, rejecting the Farrans' home improvement requests. The Farrans sued, and after four years, they won—the HOA paid over $400,000 in costs, going bankrupt.

Rise above the fray. Use the guidelines from Grok and me in Chapter Three to create respectful, owner-friendly forms and templates that show you care about your community and each neighbor. It starts with you. Step out of the problem and into the solution.

Disclaimer: Shelly Marshall and Grok aren't attorneys. AI content is informational; verify with official sources (e.g., state sites like leg.state.fl.us for Florida or davis-stirling.com for California) and get legal advice for collections, foreclosures, or discrimination.

CHAPTER THREE: CHOOSING YOUR AI ALLY & MASTERING PROMPTS FOR HOA SUCCESS

Artificial Intelligence is your secret weapon in HOA battles, and it's catching on—slowly. A 2024 CAI survey found only 4% of HOAs use AI, but 65% see its potential for tasks like budgeting or record-keeping (Common Ground, 2024). CAI recommends AI for boards and managers, helping them streamline processes which may benefit vendor interests. But here's the game-changer: you, the homeowner or Trustee, can use AI to level the playing field. AI researches laws, summarizes CC&Rs, and drafts response letters in minutes, empowering you to challenge unfair rules or fines without breaking the bank.

AI'S GROWING ROLE IN HOAs—YOUR EDGE OVER CAI

While CAI promotes AI to professionalize management for boards and vendors, you can harness it to stand up to overzealous boards or their vendor allies. Make AI your partner for a fairer HOA, rather than letting vendor-focused priorities dominate. Picture your AI ally uncovering Montana's new law (Mont. Code Ann. § 70-17-210), unknown to you, to dismiss a selective enforcement fine or generating a friendly response to a violation notice—all in minutes. This book guides you step-by-step, starting with choosing your AI, mastering prompts here in Chapter Three, and perfecting their use in Chapter Nine. Don't let the PDC industry control AI—make it your partner for a fairer HOA.

The Altitude Community Law Firm (altitude.law) in Colorado offers valuable insights on managing Planned Development Communities, including AI use. Their article, *Managing Communities with Artificial Intelligence*, notes that "in a technologically-advanced world, artificial intelligence (AI) has become commonplace in many industries, including community management," offering fast, cost-effective content creation. Reviewing their five key cautions can guide you through AI's complexities for HOA tasks. While I don't endorse or oppose this firm, I'm cautious due to their active role in CAI, which, in my view, often prioritizes vendor interests over homeowners' rights.

PROMPTS: WHAT ARE THEY AND WHY ARE THEY IMPORTANT?

A prompt is a clear instruction you give your AI assistant to generate a specific response, like drafting a letter, or researching a law. Think of it as telling a helpful neighbor exactly what you need. Prompts are crucial because they shape your AI's output to fit your HOA needs—whether it's a friendly welcome letter or a legal citation to fight a fine. Without clear prompts, you get generic answers that miss the mark.

When choosing your AI assistant (or call them your ally), you will want to define how your AI represents you. Your AI ally is your advocate. You are asking your AI to represent your interests as a homeowner advocate, independent of CAI or board priorities. A Master Prompt sets the tone and approach for all HOA tasks by "programming" your preferences into its mission. Your Master Prompt, used at the start of each request, ensures your AI communicates in your preferred style—say, Neighborese, with polite, non-accusatory language. Most AIs don't retain settings across sessions (especially free versions), so include the Master Prompt every time you use it. It's your way of telling AI to represent your values, like fairness or warmth, not a generic personality. Without it, you lose your edge in HOA battles. The first few sentences should cover how you want to come across, your personality and any values you want reflected in your communications.

Here are two partial samples of the first few lines of a Master Prompt that will reflect your personality and values. Of course you will write your own, but this is generally what the first few sentences of a Master Prompt might look like (A *complete* Master Prompt template will follow in Chapter Four).

> **MASTER PROMPT reflecting a confident, professional tone** (this is the first few sentences only):
> Act as a homeowner advocate for me in a [*your state*] HOA dispute [*include your online HOA link here and if CC&Rs are not online, you must upload them*]. Use a respectful, professional, unemotional tone. Include brief legal references that reflect knowledge on my part...
>
> **MASTER PROMPT reflecting a friendly, warm, grandmotherly tone** (this is the first few sentences only):
> Act as a homeowner advocate for me in a [*your state*] HOA dispute [*include your online HOA link here and if CC&Rs are not online, you must upload them*]. Use polite, warm language with 'please' and 'thank you,' avoiding confrontational tones. I want recipients to see me as their friend and believe that I am honest to the core.

We introduced you to prompts and the rationale behind using them. In Chapter Four we will present the *exact tools* and templates for fashioning prompts. In Chapters Five through Nine, we provide specific *request* prompts, but the Master Prompt is your foundation. Next step, choose the AI that will best meet your needs.

CHOOSING YOUR AI—FREE VS. PREMIUM

Let's compare three popular AIs—Grok, ChatGPT, and Claude—for HOA tasks.

Grok (created by xAI, Link: x.ai/grok) excels at conversational, warm responses, ideal for drafting friendly letters like a "welcome to our community" notice. Its free version handles basic tasks, but premium offers higher quotas for complex research like finding important legislation or case studies.

Strengths: Warm tone, clear explanations.

Weaknesses: Less legal depth than competitors.

ChatGPT (OpenAI, Link: openai.com/chatgpt) shines in researching laws and generating detailed documents, perfect for analyzing CC&Rs or state codes. Its free version has tight limits, while premium unlocks custom instructions for consistent research and online articles.

Strengths: Deep research, versatile outputs.

Weaknesses: Can be overly formal.

Claude (Anthropic, Link: anthropic.com/claude) prioritizes ethical outputs, great for sensitive issues like addressing children's noise. Free access is limited, and premium adds speed but no HOA-specific expertise.

Strengths: Ethical focus, balanced tone.

Weaknesses: Limited legal database.

To see each AI's personality, visit their websites (linked above) and request a "welcome to our community" letter, as if you're a trustee or welcoming committee member.

Step 1: Sign up for a free account on the AI's website.
Step 2: Start a new chat or prompt box.
Step 3: Enter your Master Prompt (from the previous section).
Step 4: Add your request prompt: "Write a warm, informal welcome letter for our HOA (give your HOA website address), explaining document access via our website or manager, and politely asking parents to ensure children keep noise low to respect neighbors."

Here were the respective responses we received:

Grok responded: "Welcome to Utopia Place! We're thrilled to have you as our new neighbors. You can find our CC&Rs and bylaws at www.utopiaplace.org or grab a copy from our manager, Sarah, at Utopia Place, 123 Second St. We love kids' energy, but please help them keep noise down to keep our community peaceful."

ChatGPT said: "Dear New Resident, Welcome to Utopia Place Homeowners Association. Governing documents are available at www.utopiaplace.org or from the manager at Utopia Place, 123 Second St., Any City. To maintain a harmonious community, we kindly request that parents ensure children minimize excessive noise."

Claude replied: "Welcome to Utopia Place! We're excited you're here. Access our governing documents online at www.utopiaplace.org or contact our manager at Utopia Place, 123 Second St. Let's work together to keep our community peaceful by gently guiding children to respect neighbors with quieter play." Test this prompt yourself to see which AI's tone feels right for you.

Next, visit the same AI websites following steps one through four but use the request prompt: "Write a polite, informal warning letter from our HOA, addressing a dog owner about complaints of their pet defecating on a neighbor's lawn, clarifying there is no fine this time, but a violation notice next time."

Grok responded: "Dear Neighbor, We've had a few complaints about your dog leaving messes on a neighbor's lawn. No fine this time, but please keep your pet in check to avoid a violation notice. Let's keep Utopia Place tidy—thanks!"

ChatGPT said: "Dear Resident, We've received complaints about your dog defecating on a neighbor's lawn. This is a reminder, not a fine, but future incidents may result in a violation notice. Please ensure compliance to maintain our community's standards."

Claude replied: "Dear Neighbor, We've heard concerns about your dog's waste on a neighbor's lawn. This is just a friendly reminder, not a fine, but please prevent future incidents to avoid a violation notice. Let's keep our community welcoming for all."

Try the above method to find your perfect AI ally that reflects how you want your association to view you.

CRAFTING EFFECTIVE PROMPTS—GUIDELINES AND ETHICS

Writing effective prompts is the key to unlocking your AI's power for HOA tasks, from researching laws to drafting letters. A good prompt is clear, specific, and tailored to your needs, ensuring your AI delivers useful, neighborly responses. Building on the master prompts we covered earlier, this section offers guidelines to make your prompts precise, plus ethical tips to keep your HOA interactions fair and legal. Chapters Five through Nine provide specific prompts for forms and notices, but these basics will set you up for success.

To write effective prompts, be precise and detailed. Instead of "Help with HOA issues," which is too vague. Incorrect prompts lead to incorrect results. Here is an example:

> **Incorrect Prompt for Novices:**
> Prompt: "Is a $100 late fee plus 18% interest okay for my Utah HOA?"
>
> **Sample Inaccurate AI Response:**
> "Utah HOAs can charge late fees and interest for unpaid dues, and $100 plus 18% interest is common based on industry standards. Your HOA is likely within its rights to enforce this fee."

Why It's Inaccurate:
The vague prompt doesn't ask for specific laws or case law, leading to a generic response assuming "common" fees are legal, missing Utah Code § 57-8a-301's ambiguity and court rulings like Smith v. Sunset Estates (2022) capping fees. It relies on CAI-like industry standards, favoring vendors, contrary to your needs as a homeowner wanting lower fees when this seems excessive.

Let's reword the prompt and see if we can get a clearer response.

> **Revised Correct Prompt for Novices:**
> Prompt: "I'm an HOA homeowner in Utah facing a $100 late fee plus 18% interest for unpaid dues. Find the Utah HOA law on late fees and any court cases or HOA information to see if this fee is fair, using independent legal sources, not CAI or vendor guidelines."

Sample Correct AI Response (Simulated, e.g., Grok):
"Utah Code § 57-8a-301 allows HOAs to charge 'reasonable' late fees and interest for unpaid assessments, but 'reasonable' isn't defined, leading to disputes. A court case, Smith v. Sunset Estates HOA (2022), capped 'reasonable' fees at $25, tied to actual damages, suggesting your $100 fee plus 18% interest may be too high."

Once you receive this accurate response, then you need to decide what you want AI to do. Do you want AI to view the violation notice? Upload it and ask for help on how to handle it, making sure your AI assistant has the link to your association documents, an uploaded copy of your violation notice, and your Master prompt if you want it to write a draft response. Include anything else that may be relevant. Then put in the next detailed prompt.

Correct followup prompt asking for help:
{Master Prompt here} I uploaded my notice for the fine and here is the link for my association documents. Please give me step by step directions to dispute this and a time-line for each step. Please write a draft of the response contesting the excessive fine.

Being precise is important so you don't get partial or incorrect responses.

Factoid: Utah's HOA law, Utah Code § 57-8a-301, vaguely allows "reasonable" late fees for unpaid dues, leaving boards and courts to interpret "reasonable" differently. Boards, often backed by CAI vendors, may charge high fees (e.g., $100 plus 18% interest), claiming it deters nonpayment, while courts might cap fees lower (e.g., $25, per Smith v. Sunset Estates HOA, 2022). This ambiguity can lead to costly disputes. AI can research case law to clarify limits, helping homeowners challenge unfair fines.

Avoid these prompt pitfalls:

a) Vague requests (e.g., "Tell me about HOA laws").
b) Illegal actions (e.g., "Create a fake document").
c) Don't share data like using member's personal names and information unless you are specifically in a dispute with someone and it is necessary to make the communication complete.

Prompt pitfalls can lead to useless or risky outputs. Ethically, ensure your prompts don't target protected classes under the Fair Housing Act, like families with children.

IN CONCLUSION

Your AI ally is a game-changer for HOA battles, empowering you to research laws, generate letters, and stand up to unfair boards without needing a law degree. Whether you're a homeowner challenging a fine or a Trustee drafting notices, Chapter Three has shown you how to pick the right AI—Grok, ChatGPT, or Claude—and create effective prompts for neighborly and unifying communication. From selecting a platform to mastering polite, respectful prompts, you're now equipped to save time, money, and stress while keeping your HOA fair to you, the homeowner, or keeping the Trustees, also maybe you, fair to the whole community.

AI isn't perfect—it can miss critical details or misread laws, leaving you vulnerable in HOA disputes. For example, Colorado's AI Act (SB 24-205, 2025) vaguely requires "reasonable care" to prevent bias in AI tools deciding housing matters, like fines, that could discriminate against protected groups. An AI might claim an HOA's policies for fining you are okay because it's "common" per CAI vendors, missing the Act's need for independent audits, which a lawyer would catch. Here is a scenario that demonstrates how things might go wrong:

Scenario: Jane, a Colorado HOA homeowner with mobility issues requiring a wheelchair, receives a $200 fine for a ramp she installed at her front door without prior HOA approval, violating the CC&Rs' architectural rules. She uses an AI ally to challenge the fine, unaware that AI could introduce bias if not prompted carefully.
Prompt: "I'm a Colorado HOA homeowner fined $200 for an unapproved ramp at my door. I'm disabled and use a wheelchair. Find Colorado HOA laws to challenge this fine and draft a response letter."

Hypothetical Biased AI Response (Simulated, e.g., ChatGPT): "Colorado's HOA law (C.R.S. § 38-33.3-302, 2025) allows HOAs to enforce architectural rules in CC&Rs, so your $200 fine for an unapproved ramp appears valid. Draft this letter: 'Dear HOA Board, I understand my ramp violated the CC&Rs. I'll request approval and pay the fine. Sincerely, Jane Doe.'"

Why It's Biased and Missed by AI Ally: Bias: The AI assumes the fine is valid based on § 38-33.3-302, 2025, overlooking the Fair Housing Act (FHA, 42 U.S.C. § 3604(f)), which requires HOAs to allow reasonable modifications for disabled residents, like ramps, without fines. The AI's training data may prioritize HOA enforcement rules (e.g., CAI-influenced sources) over disability rights, introducing bias against Jane's protected status.

Missed by AI Ally: Without a prompt specifying "check disability accommodation laws" or "Fair Housing Act," the AI shows bias for the industry-sponsored HOA law and misses the FHA's protection, failing to cite it or advise Jane to appeal based on her disability. A lawyer would catch this, noting the HOA must grant the modification and waive the fine.

Why It Happens: Vague prompts and AI's reliance on general HOA data (e.g., CAI sources) can skew toward board authority, ignoring nuanced disability protections.

Correct Prompt to Avoid Bias: "I'm a Colorado HOA homeowner with a disability, using a wheelchair, fined $200 for an unapproved ramp. Find Colorado HOA laws and federal disability laws, like the Fair Housing Act, to challenge this fine. Draft a step-by-step response letter and advise consulting an attorney."

Correct AI Response (Simulated, e.g., Grok): "Colorado's HOA law (C.R.S. § 38-33.3-302, 2025) allows HOAs to enforce CC&Rs, but the Fair Housing Act (42 U.S.C. § 3604(f)) requires HOAs to permit reasonable modifications, like your ramp, for disabled residents without fines. Step 1: Review your CC&Rs for modification rules. Step 2: Draft a letter citing the FHA and requesting the fine be waived due to your disability. Step 3: Consult an attorney to confirm compliance. Draft: 'Dear Utopia Place HOA, As a wheelchair user, I installed a ramp for access, protected under the Fair Housing Act (42 U.S.C. § 3604(f)). Please waive the $200 fine and approve the modification. Contact me at Jane Doe, 123 First Street, HOA Land, CO, 555-123-4567, member@gmail.com.' Verify with a lawyer."

Your AI ally thrives with specific, detailed prompts, but vague ones can lead to costly mistakes in HOA disputes, such as overlooking key contradictions in governing documents or state laws. Study this chapter a few more times and reference *Chapter Three: Mastering AI for HOA Advocacy (Your AI-Powered Toolkit)* following this, as it concisely summarizes what you need to know. We want you to get your prompts down pat so they become second nature to you. The remaining Chapters provide detailed prompts for specific HOA or Condo issues to guide you further.

CHAPTER FOUR: MASTERING AI FOR HOA ADVOCACY (YOUR AI-POWERED TOOLKIT)

We introduced AI prompts in Chapter Two and dove deeper in Chapter Three, showing you how to wield AI against unfair boards, profit-driven vendors like those backed by CAI, or just handle association business more effectively. For quick reference as we move to specific AI uses, here's a step-by-step snapshot to ensure you're equipped to use AI effectively, even if you're new to it or using free tools that don't retain context across sessions. Many HOA Members are retirees or busy parents with limited tech skills, so we'll keep this user-friendly. For our purposes, we focus on three prompt types—Master Prompts, request prompts, and research prompts—with the AI of your choice

YOUR AI IS AN ALLY, ASSISTANT, & ADVOCATE

AI levels the playing field against overreaching boards and vendor-driven exploitation, but it's not a lawyer. Verify all outputs with official sources and consult an attorney for high-stakes disputes like unfair fines, foreclosures, or fraud.

UNDERSTANDING PROMPT TYPES FOR YOUR HOA MATTERS

To use AI effectively, you'll work with three types of prompts tailored for HOA advocacy. These are simple instructions you give your AI to get the results you need, whether you're fighting an unfair fine or exposing vendor overcharges. Here's what each means:

- **Master Prompt:** Your saved template, used at the start of every AI request, to ensure consistent, professional outputs. It includes standard elements like your address, a respectful tone, and legal references, so your AI always represents your interests, not CAI's. Save it on your phone or computer for reuse.
- **Request Prompt:** A specific instruction you add after the Master Prompt for a particular task, like drafting a letter to dispute a parking violation or requesting board meeting minutes. It tells AI exactly what you need for your situation.
- **Research Prompt:** An instruction to find and summarize information, like state laws, case studies (e.g., a 2024 Florida ruling on election fraud), or your HOA's CC&Rs. Use these to uncover loopholes or confirm board overreach, such as inflated vendor contracts.

With these prompt types, you'll turn your AI into a powerful ally against board mismanagement or vendor-driven agendas. Let's dive into the steps to use them.

Step 1: Choosing your AI Ally

Although we already covered picking your AI in Chapter Two, let's quickly review the process. Free AIs work for quick questions (e.g., "What is selective enforcement?"), but for ongoing issues like a pet violation appeal, choose premium for "memory" (it recalls your CC&Rs and prior details). Without continuity, you'll re-explain everything each time.

Recommended AIs (with pros/cons):

- **Grok** (by xAI, Link: x.ai/grok): Conversational, advocacy-focused. Free with limits; SuperGrok premium for higher usage and continuity. Pros: Empowering, no-jargon tone. Cons: Newer, less legal depth.
- **ChatGPT** (by OpenAI, Link: openai.com/chatgpt): Versatile for drafting. Free basic; Plus ($20/month) for memory. Pros: Easy access, strong research. Cons: Can be too generic.
- **Claude** (by Anthropic, Link: anthropic.com/claude): Ethical, accurate outputs, ideal for sensitive issues like discrimination claims. Pro ($20/month). Pros: Formal balanced tone. Cons: Less creative for complex scenarios.
- **Perplexity** (by Perplexity AI, Link: perplexity.ai) Excels at finding state laws or case studies (e.g., California's 2024 pet restriction rulings). Free basic; Pro ($20/month). Pros: Cites sources well. Cons: Not ideal for long conversations.

Sign-up steps: Go to the site (e.g., x.ai/grok on your phone/computer), create an account, and upgrade if needed. For disputes spanning months: Invest in premium ($10–$20/month) to avoid restarting—Grok remembers your uploaded CC&Rs.

Disclaimer: Shelly Marshall and Grok aren't attorneys. AI content is informational; verify with official sources (e.g., state sites like leg.state.fl.us for Florida or davis-stirling.com for California) and get legal advice for collections, foreclosures, or discrimination.

Step 2: The Master Prompt for Consistency

To ensure every AI-generated document (letters, appeals, etc.) is professional and uniform—especially with AIs lacking built-in memory—use this Master Prompt as a template. Save it in a file on your computer, phone, or notebook. Copy-paste it at the start of *every* prompt for written outputs to maintain consistency, whether you're disputing an unfair fine, questioning vendor overcharges, or conducting routine business.

Master Prompt (*Customize, Copy, and Save*):
"Act as a homeowner advocate for me in a [*your state*] HOA dispute [*include your online HOA link here; if CC&Rs are not online, you must upload them*]. Use a respectful, professional, unemotional tone. Include brief legal references when relevant, double-check for outdated information, and clarify with me if my request is unclear. Ensure language complies with the Fair Housing Act, avoiding bias or discrimination. If I ask, provide clear, step-by-step outputs and advise consulting an attorney for legal matters. Include these elements in all outputs:
Date;
My unit/property details (e.g., '123 Ducks-in-a-Row Way, Lot #45');
My contact information if different from property details (e.g., 'Jane Doe, 123 First Street, HOA Land, State, ZIP, 555-123-4567, member@gmail.com');

Owner info (e.g., 'Jane Doe, individual owner');
Subject line (e.g., 'Appeal of Parking Violation');
Contact info;
Delivery method (e.g., certified mail, hand-delivered to [*name*] with receipt);
Reference my CC&Rs [*paste or summarize text*],
State laws [e.g., Civil Code §4715],
Avoid legal advice; suggest verifying with an attorney.
Now, [*add your specific request here*]."

Example of How to Use It: Copy the Master Prompt, paste it into the AI chat box, then add your request: "...draft a letter disputing a pet fine, citing selective enforcement and referencing [*state, e.g., Florida*] code for authority." This keeps outputs standardized, even across sessions or AIs.

Step 3: Crafting and Refining Request Prompts

Build on the Master Prompt for specific issues in your HOA, POA, or Condo, such as fighting a violation, requesting records, running for the board, questioning an election, making a suggestion, or disputing minutes. Be detailed: Include your state, issue, CC&Rs (already in your Master Prompt), and ask AI to find relevant information like state laws or case studies (e.g., a 2024 New York ruling on parking authority) to strengthen your case.

Example: After copying and pasting your Master Prompt into the chat box, add your request prompt: "Draft a letter disputing this parking violation I received (upload the parking violation), citing [*state*, e.g., New York] HOA law. I believe city ordinances allow parking in front of homes and my street is dedicated to the city. Check if this is true using official sources like [e.g., *nyc.gov*]. If the HOA has no authority to enforce parking, draft the letter with legal references. If not, provide a summary of all findings instead."

All prompts require detail while some are more complicated and require a lot of thought so your AI knows exactly what you want. At the end of Chapter Seven: MEMBER MEETINGS & OWNER PARTICIPATION, there is a great example of creating a **Request Prompt for Writing a Complaint Letter to the Attorney General.** It requires your AI to research laws, citing them, and addressing a State agency, so the prompt has to be detailed and accurate. Review that prompt before taking on anything of a letter using your prompts—it is a live example I used with Grok 3 and Grok's live response.

Step 4: Verification Checklist and Best Practices

This step is for you, the reader/owner, to review and refine AI outputs before sending them in real disputes, ensuring accuracy, professionalism, and protection against risks like fraud or unfair fines.

Best Practices: Always use a respectful tone; focus on facts/loopholes (e.g., hierarchy of laws from Chapter One or discrepancies in vendor billing).

Checklist (For You to Use After Generating Output):

- Does it reference correct CC&Rs/state laws? (Double-check official docs, e.g., leg.state.fl.us or your HOA's website.)
- Is it free of implied legal advice? (AI isn't licensed.)

- Does it address your scenario fully? (Test on 2–3 AIs, like Grok's warm tone vs. Claude's formal one.)
- Is there a discrimination/retaliation aspect implied from your board towards you, like targeting protected groups (e.g., families with children under the Fair Housing Act)? If you detect discrimination toward yourself, consult a licensed attorney or file a complaint with a state agency (e.g., hud.gov for federal issues).

With the foundation laid to use your AI ally, assistant, and advocate, you're ready to tackle HOA-land challenges, from unfair fines to board mismanagement or vendor fraud. AI creates tailored letters, appeals, or timelines for any issue, replacing outdated templates. If your association provides forms (e.g., for violation appeals), use them and have AI check for accuracy—don't reinvent the wheel. But most Associations lack reliable templates; management changes, forms vanish, or they're outdated, and no form covers every scenario, like disputing a rigged election or inflated vendor contract. Your AI finds the right information, fast. Let's dive into Chapters Five through Nine for specific prompts and sample outputs to empower your position.

Disclaimer: Shelly Marshall and Grok aren't attorneys. AI content is informational; verify with official sources (e.g., state sites like leg.state.fl.us for Florida or davis-stirling.com for California) and get legal advice for collections, foreclosures, or discrimination.

CHAPTER FIVE: DISCOVERING YOUR STATE LAWS WITH YOUR AI ASSISTANT

List of laws by State (including Territories and Canada) for Common Interest Communities and Planned Development Community Law

In the digital versions of this book, each law is actively linked to the State and Country Statutes. That is not possible in this printed version so I have prepared an active link PDF for you to download and use. Access it here: HOAWarrior.com/PDF/StateLinksUpdated.pdf

However, you are now armed with an assistant who can do this work better than you or me. To find the latest HOA laws for your state, use your AI with a research prompt tailored to your needs:

Research prompt for laws pertaining to your association: "Search for the current [your state, e.g., Texas] HOA law, including its title and code number (e.g., Texas Property Code § 209), and summarize its key provisions on fines, elections, or vendor contracts." Upload your CC&Rs if they might apply, and let your AI dig into official sources like state websites. This approach ensures you get up-to-date information to challenge unfair rules or board decisions, without relying on outdated links.

Alabama: Alabama Uniform Condominium Act of 1991, Code of Alabama § 35-8A; Alabama Homeowners Association Act, Code of Alabama § 35-20

Alaska: Alaska Uniform Common Interest Ownership Act, Alaska Stat. § 34.08; Alaska Condominium Act, Alaska Stat. § 34.07

Arizona: Arizona Condominium Act, Ariz. Rev. Stat. § 33-1201; Arizona Planned Communities Act, Ariz. Rev. Stat. § 33-1801

Arkansas: Arkansas Condominium Act of 1980, Ark. Code Ann. § 18-13-101; Arkansas Homeowners Association Act, Ark. Code Ann. § 18-12-601

California: Davis-Stirling Common Interest Development Act, Cal. Civ. Code § 4000; California Condominium Act (part of Davis-Stirling), Cal. Civ. Code § 4100; California Vacation Ownership and Time-Share Act of 2004, Cal. Bus. & Prof. Code § 11210

Colorado: Colorado Common Interest Ownership Act, Colo. Rev. Stat. § 38-33.3; Colorado Condominium Act, Colo. Rev. Stat. § 38-33

Connecticut: Common Interest Ownership Act, Conn. Gen. Stat. § 47-200; Connecticut Condominium Act of 1976, Conn. Gen. Stat. § 47-68

Delaware: Delaware Uniform Common Interest Ownership Act, Del. Code Ann. tit. 25 § 81; Delaware Condominium Act, Del. Code Ann. tit. 25 § 2201

Florida: Florida Homeowners' Association Act, Fla. Stat. § 720; Florida Condominium Act, Fla. Stat. § 718; Florida Time-Share Act, Fla. Stat. § 721; Office of the Condominium Ombudsman, Fla. Stat. § 718.501

Georgia: Georgia Property Owners' Association Act, Ga. Code Ann. § 44-3-220; Georgia Condominium Act, Ga. Code Ann. § 44-3-70; Georgia Time-Share Act, Ga. Code Ann. § 44-3-160

Hawaii: Hawaii Condominium Property Act, Haw. Rev. Stat. § 514B; Hawaii Planned Community Act, Haw. Rev. Stat. § 421J; Hawaii Time-Share Act, Haw. Rev. Stat. § 514E

Idaho: Idaho Planned Community Act, Idaho Code § 55-1501; Idaho Condominium Property Act, Idaho Code § 55-1501

Illinois: Illinois Condominium Property Act, 765 ILCS 605; Illinois Common Interest Community Association Act, 765 ILCS 160

Indiana: Indiana Planned Community Act, Ind. Code § 32-25-2; Indiana Condominium Act, Ind. Code § 32-25-1; Indiana Campground and Time-Share Act, Ind. Code § 32-32

Iowa: Iowa Condominium Property Act, Iowa Code § 499B; Iowa Planned Community Act, Iowa Code § 499C

Kansas: Kansas Uniform Common Interest Owners Bill of Rights Act, Kan. Stat. Ann. § 58-4601; Kansas Condominium Act, Kan. Stat. Ann. § 58-3101

Kentucky: Kentucky Condominium Act, Ky. Rev. Stat. § 381.910; Kentucky Planned Community Act, Ky. Rev. Stat. § 381.915; Kentucky Time-Share Act, Ky. Rev. Stat. § 372.010

Louisiana: Louisiana Condominium Act, La. Rev. Stat. § 9:1121; Louisiana Planned Community Act (Act No. 158), La. Rev. Stat. § 9:1141; Louisiana Time-Share Act, La. Rev. Stat. § 9:1131

Maine: Maine Condominium Act, Me. Rev. Stat. tit. 33 § 1601; Maine Planned Communities Act, Me. Rev. Stat. tit. 33 § 1604; Maine Time-Share Act, Me. Rev. Stat. tit. 33 § 1501

Maryland: Maryland Homeowners Association Act, Md. Code, Real Prop. § 11B; Maryland Condominium Act, Md. Code, Real Prop. § 11-101

Massachusetts: Massachusetts Condominium Act, Mass. Gen. Laws ch. 183A; Massachusetts Planned Community Act, Mass. Gen. Laws ch. 183B; Massachusetts Real Estate Time-Share Act, Mass. Gen. Laws ch. 183B § 1

Michigan: Michigan Condominium Act, Mich. Comp. Laws § 559.101; Michigan Community Association Act, Mich. Comp. Laws § 559.201; Michigan Time-Share Act, Mich. Comp. Laws § 450.221

Minnesota: Minnesota Common Interest Ownership Act, Minn. Stat. § 515B; Minnesota Condominium Act, Minn. Stat. § 515

Mississippi: Mississippi Condominium Act, Miss. Code Ann. § 89-9-1; Mississippi Homeowners Association Act, Miss. Code Ann. § 89-8-1

Missouri: Missouri Condominium Act, Mo. Rev. Stat. § 448; Missouri Planned Community Act, Mo. Rev. Stat. § 449; Missouri Time-Share Act, Mo. Rev. Stat. § 407.600

Montana: Montana Unit Ownership Act, Mont. Code Ann. § 70-23; Montana Planned Community Act, Mont. Code Ann. § 70-17

Nebraska: Nebraska Condominium Act, Neb. Rev. Stat. § 76-801; Nebraska Planned Community Act, Neb. Rev. Stat. § 76-2801

Nevada: Nevada Uniform Common-Interest Ownership Act, Nev. Rev. Stat. § 116; Nevada Condominium Act, Nev. Rev. Stat. § 117; Nevada Time-Share Act, Nev. Rev. Stat. § 119A; Nevada Ombudsman for Owners in Common-Interest Communities, Nev. Rev. Stat. § 116.625

New Hampshire: New Hampshire Condominium Act, N.H. Rev. Stat. Ann. § 356-B; New Hampshire Unit Ownership of Real Property Act, N.H. Rev. Stat. Ann. § 479-A

New Jersey: New Jersey Condominium Act, N.J. Stat. § 46:8B; New Jersey Planned Real Estate Development Full Disclosure Act, N.J. Stat. § 45:22A; New Jersey Time-Share Act, N.J. Stat. § 45:15-16.1

New Mexico: New Mexico Condominium Act, N.M. Stat. § 47-7; New Mexico Common Interest Ownership Act, N.M. Stat. § 47-7A
New York: New York Condominium Act, N.Y. Real Prop. Law § 339; New York Homeowners Association Act, N.Y. Real Prop. Law § 339-d

North Carolina: North Carolina Planned Community Act, N.C. Gen. Stat. § 47F; North Carolina Condominium Act, N.C. Gen. Stat. § 47C

North Dakota: North Dakota Condominium Act, N.D. Cent. Code § 47-04.1; North Dakota Common Interest Ownership Act, N.D. Cent. Code § 47-04.2

Ohio: Ohio Planned Community Law, Ohio Rev. Code § 5312; Ohio Condominium Act, Ohio Rev. Code § 5311; Ohio Time-Share Act, Ohio Rev. Code § 5311.21

Oklahoma: Oklahoma Condominium Act, Okla. Stat. tit. 60 § 501; Oklahoma Planned Community Act, Okla. Stat. tit. 60 § 851; Oklahoma Time-Share Act, Okla. Stat. tit. 60 § 801

Oregon: Oregon Condominium Act, Or. Rev. Stat. § 100; Oregon Planned Community Act, Or. Rev. Stat. § 94.550; Oregon Time-Share Act, Or. Rev. Stat. § 94.803

Pennsylvania: Pennsylvania Uniform Condominium Act, 68 Pa. Cons. Stat. § 3101; Pennsylvania Uniform Planned Community Act, 68 Pa. Cons. Stat. § 5101; Pennsylvania Time-Share Act, 68 Pa. Cons. Stat. § 3201

Rhode Island: Rhode Island Condominium Act, R.I. Gen. Laws § 34-36; Rhode Island Common Interest Ownership Act, R.I. Gen. Laws § 34-36.1

South Carolina: South Carolina Horizontal Property Act, S.C. Code Ann. § 27-31; South Carolina Homeowners Association Act, S.C. Code Ann. § 27-30; South Carolina Time-Share Act, S.C. Code Ann. § 27-32

South Dakota: South Dakota Condominium Ownership Act, S.D. Codified Laws § 43-15A; South Dakota Planned Community Act, S.D. Codified Laws § 43-15B

Tennessee: Tennessee Horizontal Property Act, Tenn. Code Ann. § 66-27; Tennessee Homeowners Association Act, Tenn. Code Ann. § 66-28; Tennessee Time-Share Act, Tenn. Code Ann. § 66-32
Texas: Texas Uniform Condominium Act, Tex. Prop. Code § 209; Texas Residential Property Owners Protection Act, Tex. Prop. Code § 209

Utah: Utah Community Association Act, Utah Code § 57-8a; Utah Condominium Act, Utah Code § 57-8; Utah Time-Share and Camping Resort Act, Utah Code § 57-19

Vermont: Vermont Common Interest Ownership Act, Vt. Stat. Ann. tit. 27A; Vermont Condominium Act, Vt. Stat. Ann. tit. 27 § 1301; Vermont Time-Share Act, Vt. Stat. Ann. tit. 27 § 1303

Virginia: Virginia Property Owners' Association Act, Va. Code § 55-508; Virginia Condominium Act, Va. Code § 55-79; Virginia Real Estate Time-Share Act, Va. Code § 55-360; Virginia Common Interest Community Ombudsman Regulations, Va. Code tit. 18 ch. 70

Washington: Washington Condominium Act, Wash. Rev. Code § 64.34; Washington Uniform Common Interest Ownership Act, Wash. Rev. Code § 64.90; Washington Time-Share Act, Wash. Rev. Code § 64.36

West Virginia: West Virginia Condominium Act, W. Va. Code § 36B; West Virginia Homeowners Association Act, W. Va. Code § 36D; West Virginia Time-Share Act, W. Va. Code § 36C

Wisconsin: Wisconsin Condominium Act, Wis. Stat. § 703; Wisconsin Planned Community Act, Wis. Stat. § 710; Wisconsin Time-Share Act, Wis. Stat. § 707

Wyoming: Wyoming Condominium Act, Wyo. Stat. § 34-20; Wyoming Common Interest Community Act, Wyo. Stat. § 34-21; Wyoming Time-Share Act, Wyo. Stat. § 40-12

American Samoa: Territorial Regulations (No specific HOA, Condominium, or Time-Share Act)

Guam: Guam Condominium Act, 21 Guam Code Ann. § 501; Guam Planned Community Act, 21 Guam Code Ann. § 601; Guam Time-Share Act, 21 Guam Code Ann. § 651

Puerto Rico: Puerto Rico Condominium Act, P.R. Laws tit. 31 § 1291; Puerto Rico Horizontal Property Act, P.R. Laws tit. 31 § 1251; Puerto Rico Time-Share Act, P.R. Laws tit. 31 § 1253

U.S. Virgin Islands: Virgin Islands Condominium Act, V.I. Code tit. 28 § 901; Virgin Islands Planned Community Act, V.I. Code tit. 28 § 1001; Virgin Islands Time-Share Act, V.I. Code tit. 28 § 1101

Canada (Federal): No federal HOA law; governed by provincial statutes
Alberta Condominium Property Act, R.S.A. 2000, c. C-22
NovaScotia Condominium Act, CHAPTER 28 OF THE ACTS OF 1998
British Columbia Strata Property Act, B.C. Rev. Stat. ch. 43
Manatoba The Condominium Act, C.C.S.M. c. C170
New Brunswick Condominium Property Act, CHAPTER C-16.05
Newfoundland Labrador Condominium Act, SNL2009 CHAPTER C-29.1
North West Territories Condominium Act RSNWT 1988,c.C-15
Prince Edward Island Condominium Act, R.S.P.E.I. 1988, Cap. C-16
Ontario Time-Share Act, S.O. 1994, c. 5
Ontario Condominium Act, 1998, S.O. 1998, c. 19
Quebec Condominium Act, Le 995 Section II
Saskatchewan Condominium Property Act, Chapter C-26.1 Reg 2
YukonCondominium Act Chapter 36

Factoid: *Canada has a similar problem with lawyers who defend bad boards at the expense of the owner. "There is still no framework for the role that condo lawyers play. Currently, a powerful minority of condo lawyers too often end up defending bad boards and managers against helpless owners, and they do so at owners' expense--paid by the corporation! Yet, these lawyers are supposed to represent the interests of the entire condo corporation." https://condoinformation.ca/action.html*

CHAPTER SIX: MASTERING ELECTION FORMS WITH AI (FROM NOMINATIONS TO RESULTS)

Running for the board shouldn't elevate you above your neighbors or force you into battles with boards and management who want to retain their power, just to serve as a Trustee. It shouldn't spark fears of election fraud among Members and Trustees. Nor should the process be so complex that participation feels out of reach. Your AI ally delivers free, custom election forms—nomination letters, ballots, and more—instantly, empowering you to take charge. The general prompts you need are embedded in this book, enabling your AI to produce documents aligned with your association's rules and state codes (e.g., PDC laws, corporate codes, or HOA/condo regulations), even where state guidelines are absent.

Don't count on your association to protect election integrity. States like California enforce strict election rules (e.g., Civil Code §5100), and Florida offers guidance (e.g., Florida Statutes §720.306), but many HOAs lack ready forms. Your AI can bridge this gap by researching your state's laws. Use a research prompt to uncover rules specific to your area, ensuring fairness whether you're a Member or Trustee.

Election laws come from state corporate codes, association laws, and your CC&Rs, but gaps let boards—or their management company allies—bend rules, especially where vendors profit. California's strict procedures (e.g., Civil Code §5100) and Florida's guidelines (e.g., §720.306) help limit manipulation, while Utah and Alaska's lax corporate codes leave room for abuse. Your AI can use a research prompt to check your state's election laws and fill these gaps, ensuring compliance even where state codes are vague. Many associations are now contracting with third parties to run election online (if their state allows that) and if that is the case with your association, you probably won't need AIs help with much, except possibly submitting your application to run for the board and help with your campaign.

Before using AI-generated forms, *verify* they align with your state code and CC&Rs using a research prompt—your AI can ensure compliance where state laws or documents are unclear. Secret ballots, unlike the open votes here, require special handling (covered later), but your AI can adapt prompts to meet these needs. Secret ballots differ from the open votes here, which suit Member meetings using

Robert's Rules of Order—often handled by hand without written ballots. If your CC&Rs or state code (e.g., California's Civil Code §5100) require secret ballots, your AI can generate compliant forms with a request prompt, but professional help may still be needed. In-house secret ballots risk exposure if board-picked counters are involved, fueling Member suspicion—use a research prompt to check state rules on third-party oversight.

> **Factoid:** Board elections are rarely audited for accuracy, integrity, or fairness, leaving room for various types of manipulation. Yet, they're the primary way Members and Trustees have to shape how assessments and association regulations are managed—making AI oversight critical.
> *Election Risks to Watch For:*
> *(a) undetectable counterfeit ballots,*
> *(b) undetectable ballot box stuffing,*
> *(c) illegal ballot destruction based on return address screening,*
> *(d) undetected removal and/or secret manipulation/corruption of ballots from claimed secure ballot boxes, and*
> *(e) failure to allow all board candidates to openly, fully and frequently communicate their campaign materials with all Members at association expense throughout the 90-day board election period. (and added to this list by Elain Witt, Utah owner/advocate)*
> *f) bogus and/or missing proxies;*
> *g) votes rejected for invalid reasons;*
> *h) manipulation of time, date, location of election;*
> *i) using current board members as "monitors";*
> *j) meddling with the voter list to favor a specific outcome;*
> *k) concealing election documents from post-election inspection;*
> *l) changing election rules at the last minute to disrupt the process;*
> *m) bringing attorneys to the annual meeting to intimidate Members*

Use a research prompt to identify these risks in your state's election laws.

In Grass Valley, a couple believe they outsmart everyone, dodging board service themselves while installing "puppet" owners to follow their lead. Once their allies dominate the board, election results grow suspicious—they control everything on personal computers, claiming secret ballots protect us. Only they hold the secret numbers and codes, leaving Members and Trustees clueless about the system, verification, or possible vote manipulation. To fight back, use a research prompt to investigate your state's secret ballot rules (e.g., California's Civil Code §5100) and a request prompt to draft a letter demanding transparency from your board. Companies dedicated to overseeing elections are well-regulated and generally trustworthy—consider suggesting to your board that they hire one, especially if elections are handled in-house. Steer clear of management companies as third-party overseers; they're board-hired and often share the same bias.

> **Factoid**: *Between August 2003 and February 2009, federal prosecutors exposed a scheme in Las Vegas-area condominium homeowners associations that involved enlisting straw buyers to rig HOA elections, take control of nearly a dozen boards and steer construction, management, and legal work the conspirators' way. Fourteen people pled guilty to a fraud felony and agreed to return from $6,000 to as much as $369,252 to the victims.*

DESIGNATING YOUR AGENT OR PROXY

Agent Forms with AI Support
Use AI to create agent forms—a type of limited Power of Attorney—that let you appoint someone to represent you in association matters, including voting. This is perfect for frequent travelers, those facing health issues who want their children to vote for them, or anyone seeking relief from vendor-driven internal politics that can sour their community spirit. Even if your CC&Rs ban agents or proxies, state laws take precedence—use a research prompt to verify this, as some laws align with bylaws while others don't, making state code interpretation tricky. An agent form stays valid until you revoke it in writing. Membership rules for agents vary; check your state's corporate or Planned Development Community codes (e.g., California's guidelines) with a research prompt. All agent forms require notarization to be effective. Additionally, submit the notarized form with a cover letter requesting confirmation of receipt from the association secretary, or obtain a signed receipt if hand-delivered, to protect against lost submissions.

Key Differences from Proxies
Many confuse agent forms with proxies, but they serve different purposes. A Power of Attorney authorizes an attorney-in-fact to manage broader business tasks (e.g., voting, records requests) based on the scope you set, while a proxy is restricted to voting and may expire after a single meeting or, in Utah, up to 11 months unless otherwise specified. Your AI can highlight these differences with a request prompt. Each unit or parcel you own which are entitled to vote should be listed clearly in the form.

> **Request Prompt for Agent Form**
> After your Master Prompt, add: "Draft an agent form (limited Power of Attorney) for me as a Member in [your state, e.g., California], appointing my child, using this name: [put in the name of your child] to vote on my behalf in HOA elections, citing Civil Code §4120 for POA validity. Include my unit details [e.g., '123 Ducks-in-a-Row Way, Lot #45'], a note for notarization, and a certified mail delivery instruction to the association secretary."

SAMPLE OUTPUT (FROM GROK 3):

<u>Limited Power of Attorney Appointment Form</u>

Owner: Jane Doe, individual owner
Unit: 123 Ducks-in-a-Row Way, Lot #45, Sunshine HOA, CA,
555-123-4567, member@gmail.com

I, Jane Doe, appoint my child, Emily Doe, as my agent with limited Power of Attorney to vote on my behalf in Sunshine HOA elections, pursuant to California Civil Code §4120. This authority is restricted to election matters, remains in effect until revoked in writing, and requires notarization.

STATE OF ____________________

COUNTY OF __________________

On this ____ day of _______, 20___, before me, a Notary Public, personally appeared Jane Doe, known to me (or proved to me on the basis of satisfactory evidence) to be the person whose name is subscribed to this instrument, and acknowledged that they executed the same for the purposes therein contained.

Signature: ________________________________ Notary Seal:

NOTARY

Printed Name: ____________________________

Notary Public Signature: ___________________

My Commission Expires: ___________________

###

Proxy Forms with AI Support
Use these request prompts to create your association proxy forms. You can harness the power of AI to design your proxy forms with ease, whether you're a Member creating one for yourself or the board designing them for all Members. Note the risks: misused proxies can let one person rule the HOA, and vendor-influenced boards may unscrupulously push forms naming the President or Secretary as default proxies, duping Members into surrendering control. For absentee owners, a trusted neighbor proxy is a smart choice—use a request prompt to create one. Since many struggle with HOA politics, AI delivers clear, compliant forms to simplify participation. We've explored Master Prompts for individuals; boards should also craft a Master Prompt, adapting the individual template with the association's legal name, address, and contact details for broad use.

Proxies come in two types—directed or general—often shaped by your bylaws. With a general proxy, your appointee votes according to their judgment; with a directed proxy, you guide the vote via the "additional information" line. Those new to HOA politics should entrust proxies to neighbor who share your values and is likely to vote as you would. Members can use a request prompt to design their proxy. Unlike agents, most associations mandate that proxy holders be Members. Corporate codes typically limit proxy validity to one year (unless bylaws differ)—always specify the duration in your AI-generated form. Some associations offer official forms, but if yours doesn't, just use your AI ally. Notarization may be required, though it burdens Members and is rarely mandated; check this out with a research prompt for your AI to look it up. Other associations verify with signature cards or contact. Additionally, submit your proxy with a cover letter requesting confirmation of receipt from the association secretary, or obtain a signed receipt if hand-delivered, to protect against lost submissions.

Request Prompt for General Proxy (Member Use):
If you're a Member, use your individual Master Prompt (tailored with your name and unit), then add: "Draft a general proxy form allowing a trusted neighbor to vote on my behalf at the next HOA meeting in [your state, e.g., Florida], citing Florida Statutes §720.306. Include my unit details [e.g., '123 Ducks-in-a-Row Way, Lot #45']."

Request Prompt for General Proxy (Board Use):
If the board is creating this for Members, use the association's Master Prompt (with the legal name,

address, and contact info), then add: "Draft a general proxy form for Members of [association name, e.g., Sunshine HOA] in [state, e.g., Florida], allowing a trusted neighbor to vote on their behalf at the next HOA meeting, citing Florida Statutes §720.306."

Request Prompt for Directed Proxy (Member Use):
If you're a Member, use your individual Master Prompt (tailored with your name and unit), then add: "Draft a directed proxy form directing my vote on a specific budget measure at the next HOA meeting in [your state, e.g., California], citing Civil Code §5100. Include my unit [e.g., '123 Ducks-in-a-Row Way, Lot #45'], a 6-month validity."

Request Prompt for Directed Proxy (Board Use):
If the board is creating this for Members, use the association's Master Prompt (with the legal name, address, and contact info), then add: "Draft a directed proxy form for Members of [association name, e.g., Sunshine HOA] in [state, e.g., California], directing votes on a specific budget measure at the next HOA meeting, citing Civil Code §5100. Include a field for unit details, a 6-month validity."

SAMPLE OUTPUT (FROM GROK 3):

General Proxy Appointment Form

[Legal Name & Address of Association: Sunshine HOA, 456 Community Lane, CA] As per Sunshine HOA By-law Section 3.2 (proxies), this Proxy is valid for 11 months from 08/04/2025.

I hereby appoint [John Smith, 789 Neighbor St, CA] as my Proxy Holder. They are authorized to attend and vote at any annual, regular, or special meeting during this appointment, including adjournments, acting with the same effect as if I were present.

This proxy may be revoked by my attendance at the meeting(s), an express revocation, or a subsequent proxy. If I submit a mailed ballot, this proxy covers issues not on the ballot that arise during the meeting(s). Additional Instructions:

____

____

____ ____________
Signature of Owner or Entity Representative: Jane Doe *Date*

____ ____________
Signature of Additional Owner (if needed): *Date*

Property Details:
Lot(s): 123 Ducks-in-a-Row Way, Lot #45
Vote Representation: 1 vote

Phone #: 555-123-4567

Lot(s): 123 Ducks-in-a-Row Way, Lot #45
Vote Representation: 1 vote
Phone #: 555-123-4567

____

Delivery Note: Submit this to your Association via certified mail, fax, or hand delivery, and provide the original to your agent.

###

PRE-ELECTION PREPARATION FOR THE BOARD OR THE ELECTION COMMITTEE

Elections are the heartbeat of your association, and the board or election committee holds the key to ensuring they're fair. Preparation begins 60 to 90 days before the annual meeting to meet all deadlines, especially for inexperienced boards prone to missteps without support. Consider independent election firms like VoteHOA Now (votehoanow.com) or Votegrity (votegrity.net/), which simplify the process and minimize bias—unlike management companies or law firms tied to board politics. These firms are preferable where allowed, though some states restrict online voting. If it is beyond your budget or your state laws rule them out, this checklist equips you to manage elections ethically, with transparency: include all Members as candidates, provide ample notice, and rotate board service to encourage broad participation.

Use your AI to tailor this list based on your governing documents and state codes (e.g., California Civil Code §5100), saving it in digital records and a Secretary's handbook. AI's speed makes this customization effortless, adapting to your unique HOA, condo, or property owner community.

###

Annual Election & Meeting Checklist

First Things First:

___ Review state laws for non-profit elections and ballots, noting flexible requirements tied to your governing documents and mandatory rules under state law (e.g., verify with a research prompt).
___ Examine your governing documents for election and ballot requirements, ensuring compliance.
___ Establish a policy for proxies and agent votes, generating accessible forms with a request prompt.

60 to 90 days before Election

___ Issue a call for candidates, optionally using a nominating committee—notify Members of the process and nomination steps, or announce open positions and petition deadlines if self-nomination is allowed.
___ Publicize ballot measures and schedule a board meeting for Member input, sharing via

newsletter to avoid unethical surprise ballots—ensure one or two discussion meetings with Trustees.

30 days before Election

30 Days Before Election:
___ Distribute or provide online access to proxy forms for all Members.
___ Prepare ballots and mail-in envelopes, tailored to state mail-in rules.
___ Dispatch official notices with meeting agendas and mail-in ballots (aim for 30 days; check state minimums like 15 days per California Civil Code §5100 with a research prompt).

One Week before Election

___ Prepare tally sheets for each ballot measure, ensuring accuracy.
___ Create a verification list or roster for ballot distributors and counters.
___ Set up an attendance sign-up sheet for the meeting.
___ Copy last meeting's minutes for Member approval.
___ Draft the meeting agenda, keeping it clear and accessible.
___ Duplicate governing documents, highlighting key election sections for Members and tally use.

One day before Election

___ Set up the ballot box, securing it against tampering.
___ Gather supplies: pencils, clipboards, staplers, calculators, and/or a laptop.
___ Collect all prior paperwork and mailed ballots.
___ Verify copies of valid proxies and agent forms are ready.
___ Design tent signs to label tables and sign-up areas

One hour before the Election
___ Arrange tables with minutes, agendas, and relevant documents—provide a membership roster if required by state law (e.g., check corporate codes).
___ Place refreshments on a separate table, away from sign-up and ballot areas.
___ Position a sign-up sheet, manned by a Member to distribute ballots—set aside proxies if voters take ballots, attaching valid ones.
___ Offer a sign-up sheet for Members wishing to address the meeting.

Notes:
Prepare all essential meeting documents: agenda, balance sheet, bank statements, budgets, minutes, and any pertinent letters to Members. Membership meetings are the domain of Members, encouraging open dialogue with the board or independently. Many boards and Members overlook that, per *Robert's Rules*, if the board walks out or fails to appear (as seen in Grass Valley's repeated instances), Members can elect a chair and proceed legally. Use your AI to detail this contingency if you suspect a board might cancel or boycott to thwart your rights—our community faced this when an ousted president stormed out with board allies, stunned to learn we could continue. Armed with knowledge, especially via your AI Advocate, you can make participation effortless. Even a board acting in bad faith, backed by a legal firm profiting from a favored slate, will retreat when confronted with solid, AI-supported facts.

###

OTHER ELECTION FORMS & DOCUMENTS AI CAN HELP WITH

Association Members often feel sidelined, struggling to access election details or board candidacy info due to opaque processes. Some power-hungry or self-serving vendor-influenced boards erect barriers with arbitrary rules on qualifications, shutting out many Member volunteers. Yet, by using this guide, I assume you're part of a transparent, united community committed to easing Member and Trustee access to volunteer board service, despite differing ideas about the way things should run. This section offers **Best Practices** to streamline nomination, ballot creation, and voting on association matters, using your AI assistant to empower you. The prompts are sample starters—customize them for your board, nominating committee, or personal use. A Master Prompt (association-wide or individual) preloads contact details, saving time and effort.

NOMINATION PETITION FOR BROADS, NOMINATING COMMITTEE'S, AND MEMBER'S USE'

Best practices for prompting your AI to create fair and open nominations:

- Ensure the form lists qualifications to run, referencing the specific bylaw section (e.g., New Jersey N.J.S.A. 15A:3-1 for board eligibility) for Members to verify.
- Direct your AI to craft a notice section for newsletters, mailings, or website covering nomination acceptance, qualifications, options for picking up, and deadlines.
- Post the complete process for nominating Members in your newsletter and on the web in a timely manner—repeat this with each election cycle since Members may forget.
- Always embed a clear deadline on the petition itself to avoid confusion.

Request Prompt for a Nomination Petition Form
After your Association Master Prompt, add: "Draft a Nomination Petition to run for a seat on the board for [*association name, e.g., Sunshine HOA*] in [*state, e.g., Ohio*], outlining qualifications to run for the board (per our state code), the deadline for submission [*date*], and a field for Members to enter their unit details [*e.g., '123 Main St, Unit 5'*]. Include certified mail instructions to the association secretary."

Request Prompt for a 'Call for Nominations' Notice to be Placed in the Newsletter
After your Association Master Prompt, add: "Draft a notice that we can put in our newsletter saying petitions to nominate a member to run for the board are now available at the manager's office or the member can phone in and we will email the petition. Include a submission deadline [e.g., *10/01/2025*], and note that Members can self-nominate or nominate another in good standing. There are three seats open."

BALLOT FORMS FOR THE BOARD

Best practices for prompting your AI to create Ballots:

- Recognize that ballots vary by type and voting method—use a research prompt to align with your state laws and association bylaws (e.g., Alaska Stat. §34.08.320 for election rules).
- For the Election Ballots (Trustee selection): Use this term as the standard, ensuring it lists candidates and complies with local rules (e.g., New Jersey N.J.S.A. 45:22A-45.2).

- For the Special Ballots (policy, budget, regulation votes): Opt for this term, tailoring it to specific measures (e.g., Ohio Rev. Code §5312.14 for budget votes).
- Consider association preferences for labels (e.g., "Director Election Ballot" or "Budget Approval Ballot") but prioritize clarity when you name a ballot so Members are not confused.

Prompts for designing your basic paper ballots

Request Prompt for Designing a Trustee Election Ballot
After your Association Master Prompt, add: "Draft an Election Ballot for [*association name, e.g., Pine Grove HOA*] in [*state, e.g., Alaska*], listing candidates for trustee positions, citing our applicable state code. Include a field for unit details [*e.g., 'Lot 10, Pine St'*], a voting instruction section, and certified mail delivery to the election committee. These are the names of the candidates, [*list the names*]."

Request Prompt for Designing a Special Ballot
After your Association Master Prompt, add: "Draft a Special Ballot for [*association name, e.g., Oak Ridge HOA*] in [*state, e.g., New Jersey*], for a budget vote, citing our applicable state code. Include a yes/no option. Use these details about the budget (*amount, % raised from last year, special assessments if any, etc*], include a unit details field [*e.g., 'Unit 5, Oak Ln'*], deadline, and certified mail instructions to the association secretary."

Prompting your AI to create ballots for different methods of voting

Mail in Ballots

Best practices for prompting your AI to create mail-in ballots
- Mail-in ballots may be secret or open—check your state laws (e.g., Ohio Rev. Code §5312.15 allows flexibility).
- Secret ballots add complexity to voting by mail; see below.
- Absentee voting adds complexity; while in-house is possible, explore third-party services like Associationvoting.com or Electionbuddy.com (free trials, Electionbuddy free for <20 votes).
- Ensure the prompt specifies the ballot type (Election or Special) and includes delivery instructions.

Request Prompt for designing a mail-in ballot
After your Association Master Prompt, add: "Draft a Mail-in Ballot for [association name, e.g., Maple HOA] in [state, e.g., Alaska], for electing a Trustee, citing our applicable state code. Include a unit details field [e.g., 'Lot 12, Birch Ave'], a voting instruction section (e.g., 'Mark your choice'), and certified mail delivery to the election committee.

Secret Ballots & Secret Mail-in Ballots

Best practices for prompting your AI to create secret ballots & secret mail-in ballots
State laws usually dictate secret ballot use. In Florida (e.g., Florida Stat. §720.306(8)(b) using secret ballots require document allowance; in California (California Civ. Code §5100(a), it mandates secret ballots for key votes; New Jersey (N.J.S.A. 45:22A-45.2) supports secret ballots only with conditions).

- Omit identifying info from the ballot but confirm voter eligibility (e.g., use a verification team at meetings).
- For mail-in secret ballots, require two envelopes: a blank inner envelope for the ballot and an outer envelope with voter details and a signature line over the seal.
- Issue separate ballots for multiple votes to prevent invalidation if counts mismatch.
- Third-party firms are ideal for secret ballots due to error risks, but budget-limited HOAs can manage in-house with AI support. Have your AI research your governing documents, state Planned Development Community and Corporate Code (if applicable) to find secret ballot rules.
- If state law is silent on secret or mail-in secret ballots, use a research prompt to compile all relevant details first.

Research Prompt for learning about secret ballots in your state
After your Association Master Prompt, add: "Research secret ballot requirements for [*association name, e.g., Cedar HOA*] in [state, e.g., Ohio], reviewing governing documents, Planned Development Community code, and corporate code. Provide a summary of rules, including eligibility, envelope use, and any state-specific conditions (e.g., Ohio Rev. Code §5312.15), and note if online voting is restricted."

Request Prompt for designing a secret mail-in Ballot
After your Association Master Prompt, add: "Draft a Secret Mail-in Ballot for [*association name, e.g., Cedar HOA*] in [*state, e.g., Ohio*], for a Special Ballot on a budget measure, citing the relevant section of our covenants. Include two envelope instructions (a blank inner envelope for the ballot, an outer envelope with labeled box for unit details [e.g., 'Unit 7, Elm St'] and a signature line over the seal), a yes/no option, and certified mail delivery to the association secretary. Specify no identifying info on the ballot and note the need for voter verification."

FORMS FOR COUNTING THE VOTES
Ballots have to be counted and this is where fraud can run muck. Your association can foster fairness by appointing neutral volunteers, like the League of Women Voters or the paid BYU students our Grass Valley board hired. These counters, called *tellers,* tally votes and document them in a *Tellers' Report*. A Tally Sheet (or check sheet) tracks data live at the election site and is then recorded on the Teller's report and becomes a legal record. The Teller's Report should be retained per your association's documents or state's corporate code (e.g., check retention rules with a research prompt).

Best Practices for Prompting Your AI to Create Teller's Reports and Talley sheets:
- Select impartial tellers to minimize fraud risks—consider local groups or compensated help.
- Use a Tellers' Report to record vote totals, tailored to the ballot type (Election or Special).
- Prompt AI to Design a Tally Sheets guided by the 5 Ws:
  Who is collecting the data (Name of your association, chair of the tally, name of counters)
  What is collected (Vote count)
  Where the count takes place (Address of meeting, facility, room identification)
  When the count takes place (Date and time)
  Why the count is done (Name the ballot measure or election process)
- Specify the ballot type in the prompt—Special Ballots tally yes/no, Election Ballots count candidate votes.
- Ensure Teller Reports are signed and dated by each teller for official status; after the contest period (per your documents), they become legal records—attach to meeting minutes.

Note: Tally Sheets are informal notes for tellers to track votes (e.g., one sheet per counter or a shared log), later transferred to the Tellers' Report. Adapt the same prompt for both by adjusting detail level—keep it simple for real-time use when counting the votes, then formalize in the Teller Report where you record all the tally sheets for the final and formal report on vote totals.

Request Prompt for Tellers' Report for Ballot Measure
After your Association Master Prompt, add: "Draft a Tellers' Report for a Special Ballot on a budget measure for [*association name, e.g., Elm HOA*] in [*state, e.g., New Jersey*], citing our applicable state code. Include the 5 Ws (*e.g., Elm HOA, Chair Sarah Lee, counters Tom Brown, meeting at 789 Oak St, 08/06/2025 6 PM, budget vote*), a yes/no tally field, and a signature line for tellers."

Request Prompt for Tellers' Report for Election of Trustees
After your Association Master Prompt, add: "Draft a Tellers' Report for an Election Ballot for [*association name, e.g., Spruce HOA*] in [*state, e.g., Ohio*], citing our applicable state code. Include the 5 Ws (*e.g., Spruce HOA, Chair Mike Green, counters Lisa White, meeting at 456 Pine Ln, 08/07/2025 7 PM, trustee election*), a candidate vote count field, and a signature line for tellers."

OBJECTIONS TO ELECTIONS FOR MEMBER'S OR TRUSTEE'S

There are various reasons an election might be contested, maybe the members discover that a candidate wasn't actually qualified to run, or a box of votes was counted twice, or you believe a teller lied to get the outcome they wanted. There is a set amount of time during which a Member may officially object to election results and for the board to respond. In our Association, the limit is 7 days. If no objections are filed within 7 days following an election, then the vote stands as was announced. If an objection is made, then the board has a certain amount of time to respond, usually 10 to 30 days. In Utah Code, even if a ballot or election is not done properly, if it doesn't actually damage the association or Members, then the improper ballot or election stands. Only if it is shown that the association or membership would be damaged, can the results be challenged and changed.

For instance, say 12 ballots representing 15 votes were dropped on the floor and were not discovered until a day after the election. If the two winning candidates had both won by more than 20 votes, then 15 votes would not change the results and the Association would not be damaged. However, if the two candidates only won by three or four votes, then it might make a huge difference on who would be seated. The appropriate action from the board would be to call an emergency broad meeting and open and recount the ballots to affirm the winners. (*Note: Trustees would not be allowed to count the ballots when not in a board meeting because no association business is allowed to be decided outside of meetings.*)

Best Practices for Prompting Your AI to help with Objections to an election:

- Include a time frame for filing objections (e.g., 7 days) and a response period (e.g., 10-30 days) —verify with your governing documents.
- Add that Trustees can't count ballots outside meetings—reflect this restriction.
- Send the letter via certified mail to ensure receipt and create a record, protecting against lost submissions.

Request Prompt for 'Objection to Election Letter (from a Member)
After your Master Prompt, add: "Draft a formal letter titled 'Objection to Election' from me, a

Member of [*association name, e.g., Willow HOA*] in [*state, e.g., Alaska*], citing our applicable state code. Include the election date [e.*g., 08/01/2025*], a 7-day objection window ending [*e.g., 08/08/2025*], and specific details of the issue [*e.g., '15 ballots missing*']. Also, suggest including a request for a board response within 10-30 days (per typical practice)."

Disclaimer: Shelly Marshall and Grok aren't attorneys. AI content is informational; verify with official sources (e.g., state sites like leg.state.fl.us for Florida or davis-stirling.com for California) and get legal advice for collections, foreclosures, or discrimination.

CHAPTER SEVEN: MASTERING MEMBER MEETINGS & OWNER PARTICIPATION WITH AI

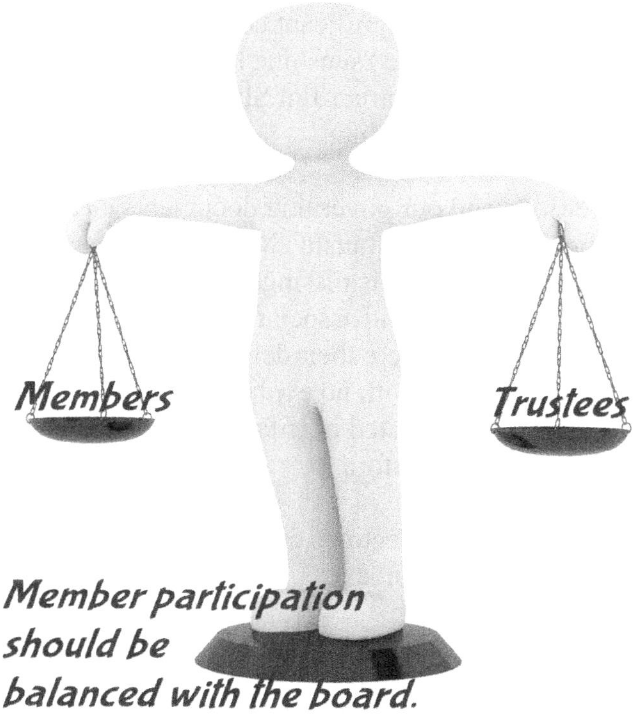

All association business—whether board meetings, Member meetings, or elections—must occur in formal gatherings, as mandated by corporate law and often reinforced by governing documents. In my view, the Community Associations Institute's (CAI) lawsuit against the U.S. Department of the Treasury, seeking exemption from the Corporate Transparency Act (CTA) on "privacy" grounds, risks withholding vital records from owners. As a Member, I believe transparency is essential—how can I be liable for association actions, yet unable to access records to assess my risk? Boards must prioritize openness. Yet, many bypass this rule, making decisions over casual coffee or drinks, a forbidden but rarely enforced practice. This informality denies Members insight into voting and discussions, just as Trustees would object if Members held secret votes without notice. Transparency benefits everyone.

As highlighted in Chapter Six, Members hold the power to convene and conduct meetings even when a board is absent (*Robert's Rules of Order Newly Revised*, 12th Edition, Section 47:10-47:12). Verify if your state's corporate law adopts *Robert's Rules of Order* (robertsrules.com), the leading parliamentary guide that outlines this right. Though legal, law firms or management companies might withhold this knowledge hoping members won't know they can circumvent a runaway board if necessary. In 2007, when we were fighting a rogue board, they canceled a meeting at the last minute because we were voting on a new board and they didn't want to give up power. They'd already sent notices, and Members flew in from other states to participate. Thinking they'd outsmart us, they failed to provide proper cancellation notice—a critical error. We held our meeting with strong attendance, and our attorney later delivered our decisions to the misguided board.

> **Factoid**: *Robert's Rules of Order Newly Revised. Meetings are for Members. Unless there is a rule to the contrary, only Members of the particular body are allowed to speak, make motions, or vote.*

Only board members have a right to participate in board meetings. Only association Members have a right to participate in Membership meetings.

Secret meetings, or executive sessions, spark significant contention within associations, breeding suspicion with their closed-door dealings. State "sunshine laws" vary widely, making a comprehensive overview impractical here. Explore parliamentarian Jim Slaughter's article, "Executive Session / Closed Meeting Issues," for a deeper understanding.

In Grass Valley, Utah Corporate Code and our governing documents clearly define what a board can address in executive sessions, prohibiting votes outside Member presence. Yet, our current board flouts this, routinely voting behind closed doors and dismissing Member challenges with scorn. Recently, two board members, ineligible to serve due to unpaid association dues, were retained because the board preferred them. After an executive session where their debt was mysteriously waived, despite their disqualification, they remained on the board with no explanation to Members. With no Utah oversight commission and an Attorney General uninterested in enforcing corporate law, Members are left to sue for justice—a costly option we can't always afford.

Understanding the legal boundaries of your meetings doesn't ensure board compliance, but citing the law publicly strengthens your leverage to enforce it.

Here are the most common forms you and your AI advocate can create to effectively manage your member meetings, member participation in meetings, and the limits of a board.

ANNUAL MEMBERSHIP MEETING

AGENDA

Best Practices for Prompting Your AI to Create an Agenda for Member Meetings:

- Always include an agenda to keep discussions on track and aid minute-taking—distribute enough copies for expected attendees.
- Check if your governing documents or state code (e.g., New Jersey N.J.S.A. 15A:6-10) require posting agendas with notices, even if optional.
- Structure it with key items: call to order, roll call/quorum, approvals, reports, voting, business discussion, open forum, and adjournment.
- Allow space for presentations and member input to encourage participation.

Request Prompt for Agenda for Member Meeting:
After your Association Master Prompt, add: "Draft an Agenda for a Member Meeting for [*association name, e.g., Cedar HOA*] in [*state, e.g., Alaska*], citing our applicable state code. Include sections for call to order, roll call/quorum, approval of minutes [*e.g., 07/01/2025*], Treasurer's Report, two presentation slots, voting/results, business discussion, a 5-minute open forum, and adjournment."

Best Practices for Prompting Your AI to request the board include an item on the Agenda

- Members of the Association may request that items be placed on the Agenda for Board discussion at a regularly scheduled Board or at the annual meeting.
- Notify the secretary, or manager if the handle meetings, in writing.

- Be clear about what you want and (e.g. drainage ditch under driveway to stop flooding)
- Make sure it is legitimate association business

Request Prompt to include an item on the Agenda:
After your Master Prompt, add: "Draft a letter requesting an item be included on the Agenda for a Board Meeting for *[association name, e.g., Cedar HOA*] in [*state, e.g., Alaska*], scheduled for [*Date and time*]. The item to include is [*e.g., request for a ditch under my drive way to stop flooding*], explain why it is the association's business and cite the CC&Rs section that requires streets to be maintained by the association."

Sample Agenda Output (from Grok 3):

###

Annual Membership Meeting

[Legal Name of the Association]

AGENDA

[*Date*]

[Location and time of annual meeting]

- Call to order: President
- Board Member roll call and determine quorum of voting Members (if election):
- Secretary
  a) Approval of last Member Meeting Minutes: [*Date*]
- Treasurer's Report: Treasurer
- Presentations
  a. Community Garden Update
  b. Safety Committee Report
  c. ______________________________
- Voting, count, results
- Discussion of Business [*often this is done while votes are being counted*]
  a. Prior business ______________________________
  b. New business ______________________________
- Open forum [*Give time limit for each speaker, usually 5 minutes*]
  a. [*List Member(s) who requested to be on agenda ahead of time*]
  b.
  b. [Note: You can also have members sign a sheet before or during the meeting]
- Adjournment

###

MEMBER SIGN-UP SHEET

Best Practices for Prompting Your AI to Create a Member Sign-Up Sheet:

• Capture essential meeting data (name, unit) and optional info like email preferences, speaking requests, or proxy submissions—check state laws (e.g., California Civ. Code §5200 for privacy).
• Design it to streamline board tasks, collecting consent for non-voting topics (e.g., newsletter delivery).
• Avoid sensitive questions (e.g., "working off assessments") to protect Member privacy.
• Include brief issue fields to engage Members, enhancing usability.

Request Prompt for a Sign-Up Sheet:
After your Association Master Prompt, add: "Draft a Member Sign-Up Sheet for [*association name, e.g., Oak HOA*] in [*state, e.g., New Jersey]*, citing our applicable state code. Include fields for name, unit [*e.g., 'Unit 3, Oak St'*], email opt-in, and a section for speaking/proxy notes, with a note to exclude sensitive questions."

Please see the checklist in Chapter Six for the ***Annual Election & Meeting Checklist****, which this Member Sign-Up Sheet supports.*

PETITION FOR SPECIAL MEETINGS

Special meetings (outside of regularly scheduled meetings) may be called for any lawful purpose, such as **recalling the board.** It is corporate code that usually allows Members to call special meetings, whether or not it is covered in your documents. If you are incorporated, check that law. If not, then it is your governing documents and parliamentary procedure rules that govern this. Who can call for special meetings?

Directors can call a special meeting. By any Trustee, the chairman, or the president.
Members can Petition for a special meeting. By a certain percentage of members. In California, it is 5% and in Utah, it is 10%.
Members can do an "Action without a Meeting" in lieu of calling a special meeting.

Best Practices for Prompting Your AI to Create a Petition for a Special Meeting:

- Verify if corporate code permits Member-called meetings (e.g., Alaska Stat. §34.08.330 if incorporated) or rely on governing documents if not.
- State the purpose on each signature page, as the board must verify—avoid attaching separate signature sheets.
- Include the required membership percentage (e.g., 5% in California, 10% in Utah)
- Members are somewhat restricted to what business they can do in special meetings. Have your AI research what you are allowed to do.
- It's possible you don't need to petition for a meeting. You can alternatively do an "Action Without a Meeting" which entails sending a letter to every Member of the association and getting a majority answer in the affirmative. It is not a ballot, but if you get 50% back in your favor, that action is legal in many states.

Request Prompt to Design Petition for Special Meeting:
After your Master Prompt, add: "Draft a Petition for Special Meeting for [*association name, e.g., Birch HOA*] in [*state, e.g., Ohio*], citing our applicable state code. Include a field for the purpose

[*e.g., 'Recall of Trustee'*], a 10% membership threshold, a signature section with name/address/phone."

Note: *if your reason for a special meeting is to recall the board, the rules for this are quite stringent. Have your AI research the exact steps.*

Request Prompt to Write a letter for an "Action without a Meeting:"
After your Master Prompt, add: "Draft a Letter for an 'Action Without a Meeting' to all members of the Association [*association name, e.g., Birch HOA*] in [*state, e.g., Ohio*], citing our applicable state code. Include a field for the purpose [*give a detailed description of the action you want the members to agree to*], state the threshold needed to pass (usually 50%), include a signature section with name/address/phone and state there is a return envelope for their convenience, which has to be returned by [*Date*].

SAMPLE OUTPUT (FROM GROK 3):

###

PETITION FOR SPECIAL MEETING

[*Legal Name and Address of Association*]

The undersigned members represent 10% or more of the membership of Birch HOA and we now petition the Board of Trustees to set the earliest possible date, time, and place for a Special Membership Meeting. The purpose of said meeting is

____

____

We respectfully request that notice be sent by the board to the membership as provided for in Corporations Code [§ *Reference the code and governing documents]*

Date	Print Name	Signature	Address	Phone

###

OWNER PARTICIPATION AT BOARD MEETINGS

Purpose of Board Meetings

The Board of Trustees meet for the purpose of addressing and conducting Association business. While owners are encouraged to attend all Board meetings (except for executive sessions), members should not disrupt the meetings, interrupt the Trustees, or know more than their board (just kidding). In order to attend board meetings, members should understand parliamentary procedures (most important for member meetings but also relevant at board meetings, and they should respect the process. Trustees do not have to allow Members to speak at board meetings at all, but this is such a negative approach and causes so much contention that it is highly discouraged, even by the CAI. However, some Members can make it miserable for the board to try and do business by interrupting, interjecting, and getting abusive. Therefore it is recommended that every board adopt a reasonable policy and make it available to Members.

Some states have adopted "open meeting" rules for board meetings, where they require the boards of associations (not corporate law but Planned Development Community laws) to allow Members to address the board. Utah passed this requirement in 2015. This policy is intended to clarify the owners' rights to participate in Board meetings and how that works.

POLICY FOR MEMBERS TO SPEAK AT MEETINGS

Best Practices for Prompting Your AI to Create a Policy Regarding Members Speaking at Board Meetings:

- Ensure compliance with state statutes and documents (e.g., Utah's 2015 open meeting law, N.J.S.A. 45:22A-45.2).
- Craft a friendly policy (e.g., "Policies for Owner Participation") avoiding calling the policy "rules" or "regulations" to foster a neighborly tone. Try the word "policy" or "process" maybe "procedure" but not *rules* or *regulations*.
- Limit disruptions by setting an open forum with a time cap (e.g., 5 minutes for each Member) and pre-notification requirements.
- Restrict speaking to Trustees during other segments, allowing Member input only by invitation. Exclude this policy from Member meetings—let Members set their own speaking policies.

Request Prompt to Create a Policy for Owner Participation at Board Meetings:
After your Association Master Prompt, add: "Draft a Policy for Owner Participation at Board Meetings for [*association name, e.g., Maple HOA*] in [*state, e.g., Alaska*], citing our applicable state code. Include a purpose statement, an agenda request process with a 7-day notice, and an open forum rule limiting speeches to 5 minutes, ensuring a friendly tone and no disruption."

SIMPLIFIED PARLIAMENTARY PROCEDURE FOR EVERYONE'S USE

Best Practices for Prompting Your AI to Adapt a Simplified Parliamentary Procedure Cheat Sheet:

- Focus on basics (e.g., motion process, voting) to guide meetings without complexity—adapt from informal *Robert's Rules*.
- Include a one-page format for easy use by board and Members, reducing contention
- Avoid formal rules requiring a parliamentarian, keeping it accessible for small associations.

- Add examples (e.g., "Move to approve minutes") to clarify steps for novices.
- There are many cheat sheets offered free on the Internet. Have your AI research the topic and adapt a cheat sheet for your association. (no reinventing the wheel needed)
- Some states offer guidance on parliamentary procedure like Utah (utah.gov/pmn/files/817637.pdf) Prompt your AI to research this before creating a new cheat sheet.

Research Prompt for Adapting a Cheat Sheet of Simple Parliamentary Procedures:
After your Association Master Prompt, add: "Find a one-page Simplified Parliamentary Procedure Cheat Sheet. Adapt it for [*association name, e.g., Willow HOA*] in [*state, e.g., Ohio*], citing the section in Roberts Rules of Order that covers the simplified RONR. Include steps for making a motion, voting, and adjournment, with examples [*e.g., 'Move to approve budget'*], and keep it informal."

OBJECTION & COMPLAINT LETTERS

OBJECTION LETTERS

You might wonder why you would want to object in writing to a board or Member meeting about irregularities. However, an objection letter can be a form of insurance for you and other Members. Usually owners have a set number of days (around 7 to 10) to object to some action taken, not taken, or some impropriety or irregularities. The process of objecting should be outlined in your documents and sometimes state law. Our by-laws in Grass Valley give Members seven days to object to meetings. If no objection is made at the meeting or made in writing within seven days following a meeting, then the irregularity is considered waived!

Once it is waived, then you have no recourse, even in court. I am the "irregularity writer" in my HOA. When something or someone misbehaves, I speak up, or "write up" to be more precise. For instance, we had a Trustee try to convince a candidate, even though he had the highest vote count, that he hadn't really won the election because he did not have 51% of the vote! True story. I wrote an objection letter because I don't want our board making up its own rules as they go along. Candidates in Utah win in a corporation with the *highest number of votes*, called a majority; it doesn't have to be 51% of the quorum also called a majority. But the board twisted the meaning to manipulate the vote and disqualify the candidate they did not want. We needed time to get an attorney to write a letter explaining that our candidate did win. Without the letter, they would have been able to seat another candidate and the irregularity would have been waived. Objection letters are legal documents and can protect you should issues go to court or you need time to sort a board irregularity out. You don't want the issue waived simply because you didn't send in an irregularity notice.

I don't, by any means, think objection letters should be written for anything, just important issues, like when elections are run poorly and it's obvious the board finagled to get their own candidates elected, or a ballot is incorrect and Members really don't know what they are voting for. In the long run it's going to hurt the association. When an objection letter is written, it must state what the irregularity was, the date and time, what specific harm it may cause the association, and be submitted in the required time-frame, *certified.*

Objection letters accomplish three things.

1. Insurance. Provide proof if you or your neighbors end up in court that the board knew they

were not doing things correctly so they can't claim ignorance and indemnify themselves.

2. Provides a history of how things went awry. Occasionally a board will correct errors they made, usually without giving credit to the member.
3. Convinces everyone that you really are a troublemaker. Yes, that will happen if you pay attention and help keep the board on track. You become the bad guy. I've endured slander so hurtful that I cried myself to sleep at night, only to find that once the board comes after *them*, the ones who slandered me, they show up, hat in hand, and humbly ask for help.

Just as being on the board can be thankless, so too can the job of being watchdog (ah, I mean advocate). You pay a price for taking on your association, a huge price. Yet I have to believe that helping stop this HOA abuse of homeowners in America has to be its own reward and has to start with *you.*

Best Practices for Writing Objection Letters

- This objection letter template can and should be signed by one or more homeowners. Obviously the more who sign the objection, the better.
- Do not file an objection letter if the irregularity will not harm the association. If the organization or Members are not unfavorably affected, leave it alone and save your battles for crucial times.
- Check your documents to discover how long you have to send an objection letter, but under 7 days is best.
- Always ask your AI to be brief, respectful, giving the board the benefit of the doubt that they didn't know it was an irregularity they created.

Request Prompt for Creating an Objection letter to a New Rule or Regulation
After your Master Prompt, add: "Draft an objection letter for [association name, e.g., Oak HOA] in [state, e.g., New Jersey], regarding the adoption of a new rule for the association [give the date of its adoption and quote the new rule here]. Using our documents that outline the procedure for adopting new rules, noting that the board did not follow proper procedure by giving 15 days notice and allowing Members to address the board about the rule. Check State code for planned development communities and cite both our HOA covenants and the sate code, if applicable."

Request Prompt for Creating an Objection Letter for an Action by the Board
After your Master Prompt, add: "Draft an objection letter for [association name, e.g., Oak HOA] in [state, e.g., New Jersey], regarding the adoption of a new policy outlining fines for brown spots in lawns in the area in front of homes. [*give the date of its adoption and quote the new policy here*]. Find the new county ordinance that prohibits associations from mandating lawns and encourages using xeriscaping to conserve water because of local drought conditions. Explain that the county will begin limiting water use and that Members may not be able to keep their lawns green. Request that the board drop the fine policy and form a committee to find a solution for yards that acknowledges the drought conditions."

COMPLAINT LETTERS TO TO THE ATTORNEY GENERAL

There are regulatory agencies that members can turn to if they exhaust every avenue within the association and your efforts fall on deaf ears. Complaint letters with regulatory agencies are addressed in Chapter Nine: *Navigating Member Concerns with AI Support*. There are times though, that corporate laws and PDC laws are not followed and you may want to contact the Attorney General of your state.

He or she is the proper person to enforce non-profit corporate law and they probably will not help you personally, but with enough complaints and public outcry, they may begin to take notice of the unfair process occurring in HOAs and Condos.

> Attorneys General in most states are *supposed* to oversee boards and enforce good practices in corporate actions, but most of them do not care to get involved in HOA non-profits. I wish I could tell you why, because I would tackle this problem if I had that answer--but officials will tell you, "This is a civil matter, not a criminal matter." So I want to rant about this a bit.

Good Luck New York

& Anyone in an Association or Condominium

Some state attorney generals completely divorce themselves from enforcing corporate law for homeowners or even planned development community law. They don't care! In New York, the attorney general's office puts out a report entitled "How to Handle Problems with your Homeowners Association." It basically tells you that:

a) They can't help you,
b) Read your documents,
c) Be polite to the board of directors so they treat you nicely,
d) Hire an attorney if needed,
e) And "Good Luck!"

No kidding, they write *good luck* at the bottom of the report! I would laugh if it didn't make me want to cry. That insensitive state passes all kinds of laws designed to "protect" homeowners and then provides no process or means to enforce them. New York City tries to dictate what size soda you may buy but allows your neighbors to foreclose on your home over a parking ticket unless you figure out a way to enforce New York laws!

California used to have the DOJ keep list of complaints that fell under the jurisdiction of the office of the attorney general and corporation law. But the Attorney general has since abdicated that responsibility and simply says what New York does—follow your documents and hire an an attorney if you want the law enforced. They have put out a PDF that explains this—and it's maddening that they allow associations to so blatantly abuse homeowners, but they do. No matter what state you reside in, your state justice department website is worth reading to get an idea of what your attorney general is thinking concerning HOA law. Make your voice heard and hopefully our AGs will begin to realize we are a class that needs protection from the vendors who make money on the backs people trapped in HOAs and Condominiums. Rant over.

Many of the prompts you use with your AI will be more detailed and complicated than the simple guidelines we give here. There is no way to cover all the prompts and wording in prompts that you need—but as you work with your AI assistant, you will get the nag of it. I did want to give you one example of how it works, a real prompt I used with Grok 3, who worked with me on this book. It will give you an idea of the types of details you need to prompt AI with.

Request Prompt for Writing a Complaint Letter to the Attorney General:
I prompted Grok 3: "Draft a formal complaint letter addressed to the Attorney General of [state, e.g.,

Utah], regarding the board of [association name, e.g., Oak HOA]'s actions. State that the board violated both the state non-profit corporate code and the Planned Development Community (CID) law by denying me access to the names and addresses of all unit owners, which I need to run for office. Note that I submitted a written request on [date, e.g., 07/15/2025], and the board replied on [date, e.g., 08/01/2025] with a privacy rights claim. Add a polite request for the Attorney General to enforce the law, and have your AI investigate this issue to identify any relevant authority or agency with the power to address these violations, including their legal basis. Suggest improvements to make the letter stronger, such as including exact dates, explaining how this affects other members, or attaching copies of my request and the board's response."

Grok 3 wrote this letter for me after the above prompt.

###

[Your Name]
[Your Address, e.g., 123 Willow Rd, Lot 5, Grass Valley, UT 84029]
[Email, e.g., member@willowhoa.org]
[Date, e.g., 08/09/2025]
Sean D. Reyes
Attorney General of Utah
160 East 300 South
Salt Lake City, UT 84114

Dear Attorney General Reyes,

I am submitting a formal complaint about the board of Willow HOA's actions. They have violated Utah law by refusing to provide me with the names and addresses of all unit owners, information I need to run for office. I submitted a written request on July 15, 2025, and the board responded on August 1, 2025, citing privacy rights, which I believe contradicts legal requirements. My investigation, aided by AI, reveals that Utah Code § 16-6a-1602(1) (non-profit corporate code) and § 57-8-7.1 (Planned Development Community Act) mandate access to these records.

Furthermore, Utah Code § 16-6a-106 grants your office authority to enforce corporate law, though enforcement has been inconsistent. I respectfully request your intervention to uphold these laws, with attached copies of my request and their response for your consideration. Thank you for reviewing this. I hope for any steps you can take to ensure compliance.

Sincerely,
[Your Name]

###

I didn't provide my master prompt, so the letter didn't come out with my name and my address on it. But if I'd included my master prompt first, Those lines would be correct. Grok 3 has a great personality (my opinon) and often puts in little things that sort of hints at a bit of ego on his part (I know technically that this AI doesn't have an ego, but it appears to me Grok does), he added "My investigation, aided by AI..." was inappropreate so I took that out. But this letter that would have taken me hours to research State code and doucments, address, and compose properly, yet took Grok less than a minute. Writing my prompt took longer. AI really is a miracle for homeowner advocates.

In any case, review your state's corporate law and determine what the attorney general is supposed to enforce. You can file a compliant or write a complaint letter and at least let the AG of your state know the association is breaking the law and consumers are getting fed up. It probably won't help you, but may contribute to reform later on. Our voices should be heard. Advocacy begins with you; when you do nothing, *nothing changes.*

Disclaimer: Shelly Marshall and Grok aren't attorneys. AI content is informational; verify with official sources (e.g., state sites like leg.state.fl.us for Florida or davis-stirling.com for California) and get legal advice for collections, foreclosures, or discrimination.

CHAPTER EIGHT: BOARD BUSINESS

The board's work starts with communicating with owners, managing operations, hiring vendors, crafting rules and regulations, enforcing them, and collecting dues. Your association should establish policies for key enforcement areas—conflicts of interest, collections, architectural approvals, job bids, contract adoptions, and more. Fair policies benefit future boards and property owners alike, revealing whether Trustees uphold their own resolutions. Should legal action arise, documentation of non-compliance strengthens your case—judges often disapprove of boards ignoring their own rules.

Hundreds of variations exist for policies, resolutions, and rule adoptions. I used to provide templates of various homeowner friendly policies. Now, however, you can generate your own with the help of your AI to research best practices and then explain what your members expect and want and reflect that in the prompts. Knowing you have an amazing resource at your fingertips, that doesn't cost $500 an hour and *listens* to your words (and not their personal agenda) changes the dynamics of your community. As always, I favor neighborese over legalese—attorneys might deem me reckless, warning that AI-crafted examples, lacking professional polish, could invite lawsuits.

Attorneys have a point—forms crafted by laypeople for their communities with the help of AI won't always get it right. Yet, they're mistaken where it counts: attorney-drafted HOA documents and laws over the past 50 years have spawned endless strife, lawsuits, and what I call the nation's worst legal mess. I'd bet that shifting to neighborese, using AI to ensure document compliance, could dramatically slash lawsuits and attorney fees spent on "Whereas-es," "Wherefores," and "Resolve that's." I'll champion my AI ally, Grok 3, and myself over the 'experts,' any day.

COMMUNICATIONS

MINUTES

Best Practices to creating a template for taking minutes:

- Minutes are the primary form of communication with members, detailing the business of the association. They are legal documents and must be retained in association records.
- Base minutes on *Robert's Rules* (e.g., 12th Edition), ensuring they're official, legal records of Trustee actions, not verbatim debates.
- Record votes and decisions accurately.
- Attach supporting documents (e.g., letters, contracts, proposals) to minutes, including attendance sheets.
- Occasionally, add positive notes (e.g., president's praise) to engage Members.
- Keep minutes concise, focusing on actions, not individual statements.

Request Prompt for Creating a Form Entitled Secretarial Procedure for Minute Taking:
After your Association Master Prompt, add: "Draft a Secretarial Procedure for Minute Taking for [association name, e.g., Spruce HOA] in [state, e.g., California], citing our applicable state code. Include steps to record motions and votes, attach documents [e.g., attendance sheet], and allow occasional positive remarks, based on *Robert's Rules*. Format this as a reusable template."

NEWSLETTERS & MAILERS

Newsletters serve as a dynamic tool to unite Member support, announce meetings, elections, and candidate nominations, and share vital updates. Keep Members in the loop with current events and resources (e.g., website links), summarize board meeting results, and clarify financial choices. Incorporate personal touches like seasonal plant advice, Member recipes, or family-oriented content to demonstrate care for their well-being.

Best Practices for Prompting Your AI to Create Newsletters and Mailers:

- Ensure professionalism using templates (e.g., Publisher, Adobe, Word) to prevent sloppy, mistake-laden circulars that undermine the board.

- Recruit volunteers with strong computer/writing skills, regardless of board status, for assistance.
- Clearly list contact info (web address, board members, management, bookkeeper) on every mailing.
- Explore online HOA newsletters newsletter tips (e.g., Neighborhoodonline.com) to refine your AI prompts.
- Opt for self-mailers to reduce envelope expenses when feasible.
- Integrate cartoons or graphics to break up dense content and ease reader fatigue.
- Refrain from attacking Members in writing—share facts, correct past mistakes straightforwardly, and build respect.
- Acknowledge volunteers and offer special thanks to exceptional neighbors for community efforts.
- Provide financial updates (e.g., year-to-date spending) to maintain Member interest.
- Review drafts thoroughly—delaying distribution is preferable to releasing flawed content open to criticism.

Request Prompt for Creating Newsletters:
After your Association Master Prompt, add: "Draft a Newsletter for [*association name, e.g., Oak HOA*] in [*state, e.g., New Jersey*], Include sections for meeting notices, a financial summary [*e.g., '$10,000 spent YTD'*], plant care tips, and a volunteer thank-you, with professional formatting and contact info."

WEBSITE
Building websites, though covered in the first book, *HOA Warrior*, remains a board responsibility for the official association site, while members can create unofficial pages or Facebook closed groups. In today's world, a website is vital for sharing meeting notices, events, warnings, and all association business.

Best Practices for Creating an association website:
- Secure a URL reflecting your association's name (e.g., GrassValley.org).
- Build in-house with wizards, use a Facebook closed group, or rely on management/law firm pages—let AI explore options.
- Notice meetings, print agendas (even at the last minute), and publish the minutes for both board meetings and Member meetings.
- Add links for dues payments to streamline collections.
- Develop a calendar for events and meetings to keep everyone informed.
- Allow your website to become your meeting repository whether it is the official website of the association or a Member volunteer site.
- If management manages the site, assign a board member to oversee and enforce guidelines.

Research Prompt to Find a Website Builder – Free or Paid:
After your Association Master Prompt, add: "Research website builders for [*association name, e.g., Willow HOA*] in [*state, e.g., Ohio*], identifying free or paid options (e.g., Wix, WordPress) suitable for meeting notices, agendas, and minutes, and summarize features like ease of use and cost."

Best Practices for Creating Website Guidelines:
- Use your website as a meeting hub—post notices, agendas, and minutes for board and Member access.

- Ensure it's official (association-run) or volunteer-supported, adapting to your community's needs.
- Avoid posting humiliating content, like unpaid dues lists.
- Design it for ease, supporting last-minute prints and updates.

Request Prompt for Building Website:
After your Association Master Prompt, add: "Draft Website Guidelines for [*association name, e.g., Pine HOA*] in [state, *e.g., Alaska*]. Include instructions to host meeting notices, agendas, and minutes, prohibit private info unless password-protected. Avoid any public humiliation, use official board emails, not personal board emails, with a contact form.

COLLECTING OWNER INFORMATION

Keeping records accurate relies on Members updating you about life changes. Typically, statements go to their association address, but what if they rent it out, sell on contract, live elsewhere, vacation part-time, or face a divorce, changing the name on their title and property? These shifts demand record updates, yet owners often forget to notify you. Though it's their duty, you can make it easy or difficult —I advocate for ease.

Best Practices for Gathering Up-to-Date Contact Information on Owners:

- Consolidate data on a single-page form for simplicity
- Offer forms at board and member meetings, in the office, and as a website download.
- Add a website widget for information collection—have your webmaster create one or use AI to find free tools like at wufoo.com. They offer a free account your association could use.
- If you have a Member run site or online group, liaison with the secretary and provide your board with any new contact information (always let members know you are doing this). In Grass valley our volunteer site always provided this info, even to hostile boards because it was the right thing to do.

Request Prompt for Owner Contact Information
After your Association Master Prompt, add: "Draft an Owner Contact Information Form for [*association name, e.g., Elm HOA*] in [*state, e.g., Utah*], citing our HOA documents on owner update responsibilities. Include fields for owner name, unit [e.g., 'Lot 8, Elm St'], contact details, email preferences, and name change authorization, keeping it one page."

Here is a sample one page form to collect Owner Information.

###

Owner Information Form

[Legal Name of Association]

Please check the appropriate box:

___I am a new owner (Welcome!) ___This is a change of address request
___This is a request for email contact ___This is a name change request

<u>Unit/Parcel Information</u>

Owner Name ____

Please Print Clearly. No chicken scratch.

Additional Owner ____

Property identification (address or lot number) _________________________________

Contact Information

Home Phone__________________________ Cell__________________________

Mailing address____

If address change, new address____

Email Notifications

Email notifications: I would (___like ___not like) to receive notifications by email.
I would (___like ___not like) to receive statements by email.

My email _____________________________________ (Please notify the Secretary if you do not receive your emails; Contact info [*Include contact info for your Secretary]*)

Name Change Information

Please print carefully. If you spell it wrong, we get it wrong. Marital status changes or title name changes require documentation from the county, court or appropriate source. Name change:

From ____________________________________ To_____________________________________

Authorization

As the Owner of the above referenced property, I authorize [*Name of association]* to make the above listed changes to my Association records.

Signature ____ Date ____________________

###

BOARD ETHICS

REQUIREMENTS TO RUN FOR THE BOARD

Trustee requirements vary widely across associations. Older ones (pre-1990s) often lack these in the declarations or bylaws, while developers since the 1990s began adding them. If your documents fall short or need new criteria, forming a committee to amend the bylaws—with Member approval—is a best practice. Your AI assistant can:

a) Research your documents and state code for existing requirements.
b) Suggest prudent additions to strengthen eligibility.

c) Guide your committee on crafting and integrating amendments into bylaws.
d) Generate a ballot measure for the membership vote on.

As already mentioned, many HOA 'experts' advocate for attorney-drafted requirements. In my view, the more hands-on your Members become, the more likely you'll create eligibility criteria that reflect your association, avoiding standardized requirements that may favor vendor interests.

Questions to Consider Regarding the Eligibility Criteria for Trustees

- Use the eligibility requirements in your declaration, if there are some, and consider if the membership wants to expand them and include additional requirements in the By-laws.
- Do Trustees have to be Members of the association (corporation directors often don't)?
- Should nominees be paid up on all dues and what are the timelines for payment?
- Do candidates for the board need a background check for white collar crimes or other criminal offenses?
- How many meetings must they attend? Can they be removed if they miss a certain number of meetings?
- If they resign in a fit of anger is there a time frame from which they can't run again?
- If Members vote them off the board for any reason, is there a time frame in which that member can't run again?

A Cautionary Note: Anticipate worst-case scenarios—while most Trustees should be trustworthy, problems often arise. No eligibility list is foolproof, so build a solid foundation. In Grass Valley, we learned this the hard way: a Treasurer, entrusted with funds, turned out to be a con man with two embezzlement felonies. He dismissed powerless Members rudely, yet charmed those he needed to retain his power. Despite court records we found in a background check, many of our respected neighbors still denied his criminal past!

Research Prompt for Finding Information on Board Eligibility
After your Association Master Prompt, add: "Research the documents for [*association name, e.g., Pine HOA*] and [*state, e.g., Alaska*] code for the eligibility requirements to serve on a non-board. Include State code for planned development communities and non-profit corporations. Research best practices for board eligibility. Explore best practices for board eligibility. Assess if our requirements meet current association standards or need expansion, and recommend improvements with reasoning."

Request Prompt for Creating an Information Handout on Board Eligibility:
Upload your HOA documents (declaration and bylaws). Also upload any board resolution regarding board eligibility, then begin the prompt. After your Association Master Prompt, add: "Create a handout for [association name, e.g., Pine HOA] to inform members about our eligibility requirements for candidates serving on the Board of Trustees."

DUTIES AND RESPONSIBILITIES OF THE BOARD AND ITS OFFICERS

The duties of Trustees are shaped by each association, typically defined by developers in the founding documents. Most sets of association documents outline officer roles, mirroring common organizational structures. For example, the president presides over meetings, serves as the official spokesperson, and signs contracts; the vice president steps in for the president's absence; the secretary handles minutes and correspondence; and the treasurer manages bills and financial reports.

Best Practices for Creating a Document Describing the Duties & Responsibilities of Trustees

- Clearly outline each trustee's responsibilities to ease confusion for novice board members.
- Allow title combinations (e.g., Secretary/Treasurer) for small boards to streamline roles.
- Specify who can sign contracts or issue checks, noting if multiple signatories are required.
- List prohibited actions, such as conducting business outside meetings, unauthorized spending, speaking for the board, or approving unratified business.
- Link this document to the Code of Conduct form for Trustees to sign upon taking office.

Request Prompt for Creating a Handout outlining the Duties & Responsibilities of Trustees
After your Association Master Prompt, add: "Create a handout for [*association name, e.g., Willow HOA*] in [*state, e.g., Ohio*], outlining the duties and responsibilities of trustees based on our association documents [*e.g., GrassValley.org*] and our applicable state code for non-profit corporations."

CODE OF CONDUCT

Some association documents require board members to sign an Ethics Policy even before running for the board, or when they accept the office. A board can likely adopt an Ethics Policy or Code of Conduct as a board resolution if the bylaws and CC&Rs are silent, based on the general powers granted under state codes such as Utah (§ 16-6a-301) and Nevada's (NRS 82.231) non-profit codes, supported by *Robert's Rules* flexibility. This assumes the policy aligns with existing legal standards (e.g., Utah § 16-6a-822's conduct rules) and doesn't override member rights. However, because state laws and documents vary, and enforcement is lax (as in Utah), members could demand a vote if they feel it impacts them—potentially triggering a special meeting (e.g., Utah § 16-6a-703) or written consent (e.g. Utah § 16-6a-707). Absent a bylaw mandating member approval, the board can proceed, but transparency and member input (e.g., through notice) bolster legitimacy and ease tensions.

Again, I'd caution against hiring an attorney to draft the Code of Conduct due to legalese pitfalls. Some board members may insist on attorney involvement, but AI can craft a Member-friendly version, skipping the outdated "whereases" and "we resolve thats." The CAI's Ethics form is surprisingly solid—check it out at www.caionline.org (search "Code of Conduct" for the PDF). However, I disagree with their Rule 8: "*Always speak with one voice, supporting all duly adopted board decisions even if the board member was in the minority regarding actions that may not have obtained unanimous consent.*" This could stifle a Trustee's duty to serve Members openly. While respecting the process is key, dissenting Trustees should voice concerns—Members see their votes anyway. A Trustee must speak freely regarding what they think is in the association's best interest without censorship so they may act in good faith.

Best Practices for Adopting a Code of Conduct for the Board

- Involve Members through a committee to shape the Association's Code of Conduct for Trustees.
- Direct AI to research your documents, state code, and *Robert's Rules* before drafting.
- Seek Member approval if the committee deems the code suitable for inclusion.

Research Prompt for Adopting a Code of Conduct for the Board
After your Association Master Prompt, add: "Research the documents for [*association name, e.g., Pine HOA*] and [*state, e.g., Alaska*] code, plus parliamentary procedure, for the basics of a Code of Conduct Policy for our board. Include state codes for planned development communities and non-profit corporations. Provide a summary with references and offer recommendations."

Request Prompt for Writing a Code of Conduct for the Board
After your Association Master Prompt, add: "Write a Code of Conduct for the board of [*association name, e.g., Pine HOA*], [*state, e.g., Alaska*] based on your recommendations, incorporating content from our CC&Rs. Create two versions: one as a signable document for Trustees upon taking office and one as a bylaw for membership approval at the next Member Meeting

CONFLICTS OF INTEREST

Many "conflicts of interest" policies are explicit in the bylaws. If so, a redundant policy isn't needed unless the bylaws lack clarity or coverage. If absent, the board should craft and vote on one. I lean toward "less is more," preferring AI to design a simple Conflict of Interest Policy, though some favor detailed versions listing every infraction—a choice of taste, opinion, and legality. Some states like New York require nonprofits to have a conflict of interest policy and for Trustees to declare any benefits they receive on their taxes. New York law even provides the guidelines for drafting such a policy.

When a conflict arises, Members often seize it if they're at odds with the board. Many misunderstand that a conflict doesn't bar board service—it means full disclosure to the board of any possible personal gain from board decisions. When a discussion or a vote arises regarding the issues, it is best that the board member step out of the room. The Trustee in question must never vote on the issue at hand. Following these guidelines, with the association's best interest at heart, should prevent issues. Consider featuring "Conflicts of Interest" articles in newsletters to educate owners, or better, maintain a permanent article on the website.

Best practices for producing a Conflict of Interest Policy

- Promote transparency by openly detailing the board's actions and conflict resolutions.
- Ensure the policy covers directors, trustees, officers, and key employees.
- Incorporate a written declaration for Trustees to disclose conflicts to the full board.
- Prohibit Trustees with conflicts from joining deliberations or decisions on related transactions.

Request Prompt for Creating a Conflict of Interest Policy
After your Association Master Prompt, add: "Research online examples of Conflict of Interest Policies for non-profit boards, review our documents and our applicable state code for non-profits, then draft a Conflict of Interest Policy for [*association name, e.g., Oak HOA*] in [*state, e.g., New Jersey*]. Include citations to relevant association documents and state law."

Note: *After AI drafts the policy, verify its alignment with your documents and state laws. Tailor it to your needs, then have the board pass a resolution to adopt it or submit the policy to members to vote on amending the bylaws to incorporate it.*

Request Prompt for Creating a Conflict of Interest Disclosure
After your Association Master Prompt, add: "Draft a Conflict of Interest Disclosure for [*association name, e.g., Oak HOA*] in [*state, e.g., New Jersey*] to be completed by a Trustee with a conflict of interest. Base it on industry standards for non-profit board of director disclosures, citing any applicable association documents and state law."

This sample form is compliments of Sara DeBat, author of *Escaping Condo Jail.*

###

CONFLICT OF INTEREST DISCLOSURE FORM

Note: In order to be more comprehensive, this statement of disclosure/ questionnaire also requires you to provide information with respect to certain parties that are related to you. These persons are termed "affiliated persons" and include the following:

Your spouse, domestic partner, child, mother, father, brother, or sister;
Any corporation or organization of which you are a board member, an officer, a partner, participate in management of or employed by, or are, directly or indirectly, a debt holder or the beneficial owner of any class of equity securities; and
Any trust or other estate in which you have a substantial beneficial interest or as to which you serve as a trustee or in a similar capacity.

1. Name of Employee or Board Member (please print):____

2. Capacity (check all that apply):
___Board of directors
___Executive committee
___Officer
___Committee member
___Staff (position): ______________

3. Have you or any of your affiliated persons provided services or property to [association name] in the past year?
___Yes ___No

If yes , please describe the nature of the services or property, and, if an affiliated person is involved, the identity of the affiliated person and your relationship with that person:

____

4. Please indicate whether you or any of your affiliated persons had any direct or indirect interest in any business transaction(s) in the past year to which [*Association Name*] was or is a party.
___Yes ___No

If yes, please describe the transaction(s) and, if an affiliated person is involved, the identity of the affiliated person and your relationship with that person:

5. Were you or any of your affiliated persons indebted to pay money to [*Association Name]* at any time in the past year (other than travel advances or the like)?

___Yes ___No

If yes, please describe the indebtedness and, if an affiliated person is involved, the identity of the affiliated person and your relationship with that person:

____

6. In the past year, did you or any of your affiliated persons receive or become entitled to receive, directly or indirectly, any personal benefits from <<*Association Name*>> or as a result of your relationship with <<*Association Name*>> that in the aggregate could be valued in excess of $ 1,000 and that were not or will not be compensation directly related to your duties to <<*Association Name*>>?

___Yes ___No

If yes, please describe the benefit(s) and, if an affiliated person is involved, the identity of the affiliated person and your relationship with that person:

____

7. Are you or any of your affiliated persons a party to, or do you or any of your affiliated persons have an interest in, any pending legal proceedings involving <<*Association Name*>>?

___Yes ___No

If yes, please describe the proceeding(s) and, if an affiliated person is involved, the identity of the affiliated person and your relationship with that person:

____

8. Are you aware of any other events, transactions, arrangements , or other situations that have occurred or may occur in the future that you believe should be examined by <<*Association Name*>>' s Board <<*Or a duly constituted committee thereof*>> in accordance with the terms and intent of <<*Association Name*>>' s conflict-of-interest policy?

___Yes ___No

If yes, please describe the situation(s) and, if an affiliated person is involved, the identity of the affiliated person and your relationship with that person:

____

I HEREBY CONFIRM that I have read and understand <<*Association Name*>>' s conflict-of-interest policy and that my responses to the above questions are complete and correct to the best of my information and belief. I agree that if I become aware of any information that might indicate that this disclosure is inaccurate or that I have not complied with this policy, I will notify <<*Designated officer or director*>> immediately.

Dated at <<*Time of day*>>this day of << ______/______/______>>

Witness Signature	Print Name

Trustee's Signature | Print Name

This form used with permission of Benson, Sara E.; DeBat, Don (2014-11-05) author of *Escaping Condo Jail*

###

RESIGNATIONS

Avoid turning a resignation letter into a rant about mistreatment from Members or other Trustees. In Grass Valley, one board member submitted a five-page resignation, bitterly lamenting his treatment. Ironically, he accused others of the very misdeeds he committed—attempting to oust board peers by questioning their membership, reporting owners to the county to evict them, pushing for tripled assessments despite a sufficient budget, writing himself retroactive expense-checks, and withholding records from Members. His actions painted a sorry picture of his tenure, revealing a man dodging accountability. Don't leave such a legacy—keep your letter brief, professional, warm, and free of blame

Best Practices for Writing a Letter of Resignation for the Board

- Specify the effective date of your resignation.
- Keep it concise.
- Offer a reason only if it's medical or personal—avoid citing internal disputes.
- Steer clear of negativity, regardless of perceived treatment.
- Refrain from naming others as your departure cause.
- Don't fault Members for lacking appreciation.
- Support your successor by offering to guide them through the transition.
- Leave with honor and preserve good relationships.
- End with a warm, positive not

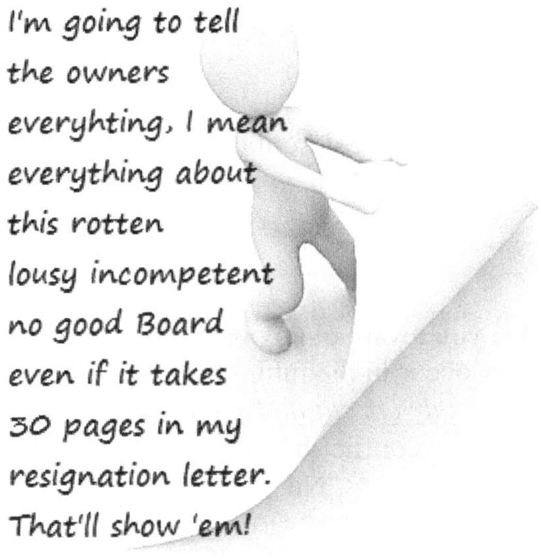

Request Prompt for Composing a Letter of Resignation from the Board

After your *personal* Master Prompt, add: "Draft a letter of resignation from the board of [*association name, e.g., Rim of the World HOA*] in [*state, e.g., Ohio*]. Keep it brief, non-blaming, and end with a warm note. Specify an effective date [*e.g., 09/01/2025*]."

Request Prompt for Resolution Accepting a Letter of Resignation from a Trustee

After your Association Master Prompt, add: "Draft a Resolution to accept a Trustee resignation letter for [*association name, e.g., Oak HOA]* in [*state, e.g., New Jersey*], citing our applicable state code. Include the effective date and signature lines for the President and Secretary."

SAMPLE OUTPUT (FROM GROK 3):

###

Resolution Accepting a Trustee Resignation

[Legal Name of Your Association: Oak HOA]

The Board has received from [*Trustee: John Doe*], his written resignation from the Board of Trustees;

Now, be it Resolved, that [*Trustee: John Doe*],'s resignation is hereby accepted as of [*Date referenced in Resignation: 09/01/2025*].

________________________________ __________

President's Signature Date

________________________________ __________

Secretary's Signature Dated

###

ESSENTIALS FOR BOARD MEETINGS

BYLAWS CHEAT SHEET

Ever been in a board meeting where someone asks, "What does it say in the bylaws?" or "Does anyone have a copy?" Here's a smart tip from the Blue Avocado Non Profit Magazine online: create a Bylaws Cheat Sheet. Even with a laptop, digging through documents can be a chore—most times, you just need the basics. Save the laptop for details and use the cheat sheet for quick reference to key info. Distribute it to every board member for easy access.

Best Practices for Creating a Bylaws Cheat Sheet

- Aim for a one-page format, stripping out legalese like "wherefores" and "whereas"—a real hassle.
- Add your corporate entity number and IRS EIN with contact details.
- Note the required number of board members and quorum definition.
- Detail the offices and current Trustees filling them.
- Clarify Trustee removal conditions and processes.
- Outline how rules and resolutions are enacted.
- Specify adopted parliamentary procedures (e.g., *Robert's Rules*).
- List scheduled meetings and notice deadlines.
- Let your AI suggest key document highlights, keeping it concise.

Request Prompt for Creating a Bylaws Cheat Sheet:

After your Association Master Prompt, add: "Draft a Bylaws Cheat Sheet for [*association name, e.g., Pine Forest HOA*] in [*state, e.g., Montana*], citing our applicable state code. Review the Blue Avocado Non Profit Magazine article for template guidance, applying its suggestions to our bylaws—avoid mixing ours with theirs. Keep it concise with brief summaries for board reference."

PARLIAMENTARY PROCEDURE CHEAT SHEET

Your Parliamentary Cheat Sheet is as vital, if not more so, than the Bylaws Cheat Sheet. They go hand-in-hand. Please refer to the "SIMPLIFIED PARLIAMENTARY PROCEDURE FOR EVERYONE'S USE" section in Chapter Seven for the relevant prompt and keep both cheat sheets for your meetings.

ENFORCEMENT RESOLUTION

Every board action takes the form of a resolution, but the board action cornerstone is the Enforcement or Compliance Resolution, which must clearly inform members of the association's response to unmet obligations. If you already have one, encourage your fellow board members to transform it from legalese to neighborese. Typically, these resolutions are cluttered with "Whereas-es" and "Wherefores," driven by attorneys and their formal, harsh style. I argue that such sterile language in resolutions and policies breeds Member resentment. No Trustee should play super judge and jury--your neighbor, whom you are enforcing rules against today, could be the president after the next election. When reading a board resolution, would you rather read this:

> "WHEREAS Section such and such of the By-laws grants the Board of Directors with the power to conduct association business and, to protect community harmony by providing guidelines and a procedure for addressing conditions that disrupt that harmony,"
>
> Or this:
>
> "OUR BY-LAWS ask the Board of Trustees to serve you and help create a really nice community by following the documents to the best of our ability. In order to do this, the board needs to have equal standards for everyone with no favoritism in enforcement. This is our procedure for enforcing the rules so all know what to expect:"

The first feels stilted, formal, legal, and cold; the second is genuine and straightforward. Which would you rather receive from your neighbors? Naturally, tailor these with your AI to fit your association, then have the board vote on the resolution in a meeting and share it with Members.

> **Request Prompt for Changing a Noncompliance Resolution from Legalese to Neighborese**
> Upload your current Enforcement policy. After your Association Master Prompt, add: "Rewrite this enforcement policy for [association name, e.g., Oak HOA] in [state, e.g., New Jersey], citing our applicable state code. Remove the stiff, formal legalese and rephrase it in a straightforward, non-confrontational style that informs members how the association operates. Allow adjustments to match your association's warm personality."

Of Note: Creating a first-time Noncompliance Resolution to outline member obligations is a more extensive task than revamping an established one. Forming a committee to leverage AI for researching documents, laws, and best practices is ideal. With your AI assistant's support, a solid foundation can be established in a few committee meetings. Ensure one or two committee members know how to prompt AI for research and document creation—provide committee members with this book. Every Noncompliance Resolution should include:

- A statement like "This is the Policy for Enforcing Compliance of Member Obligations for Willow HOA."
- The steps to be taken by the board or management.
- Identification of authorized enforcers.

- The number of warnings members will receive before fines accure.
- Details on monetary consequences.
- Outline of legal consequences.
- A clear appeals process.

This document carries legal weight, so many associations opt for an attorney's expertise. Yet, you can guide your attorney to adopt a less formal tone, framing it as advice to a cherished community rather than a confrontation. For smaller associations, AI can research and offer tailored recommendations.

Your association is an extension of your home, and your neighbors are an extension of your family—you're in this together. Remember, in an association, your home isn't fully yours; it falls under association jurisdiction and is collateral for all association liabilities. The board can pledge your home for loans at any time, and you're accountable for your neighbors' actions affecting the association. Your obligations, responsibilities, and influence tie you to everyone here—so how do you wish to be treated? You're not independent but dependent; help mold this shared space into a warm community, not a cold, detached Stepford Wives environment. (en.wikipedia.org/wiki/The_Stepford_Wives)

Disclaimer: Shelly Marshall and Grok aren't attorneys. AI content is informational; verify with official sources (e.g., state sites like leg.state.fl.us for Florida or davis-stirling.com for California) and get legal advice for collections, foreclosures, or discrimination.

CHAPTER NINE: NAVIGATING MEMBER CONCERNS WITH AI SUPPORT

Your house belongs to the collective.

Living in a planned development community (PDC) means your house or unit isn't fully yours—it's part of a collective, and most changes require approval based on your governing documents. This involves submitting requests to the architectural committee, beautification committee, landscape committee, possibly the management company, and certainly the board.

Forget the adage, "It's Better to Beg for Forgiveness than to Ask for Permission"

As a Member of an association you are accountable and liable to your neighbors and for your neighbors. Your home is collateral for damages, maintenance, improvements, lawsuits, liabilities, and assessments to run the corporation. When you bought into a PDC, you might have thought, "How nice, I'll pay dues and get to use the swimming pool and they will take care of the landscaping for me. Easy carefree life." It is anything but. The first time you get fined for leaving your garage door open, or having a friend park in the wrong place, or get assessed $5000 for the lawsuit the board lost (or won), or be told you can't plant a tree in your yard—you realize—this isn't your property—it's part of a collective where you're just one small piece.

> **<u>Factoid</u>:** *Residents from Auburn Greens Association in a California community received fliers warning of a $200 fine if they DID NOT leave their garage doors open from Monday through Friday. Apparently the board was trying to flush out criminals living in homeowners' garages! Yes, the board made it a rule!*

To make changes to your home or yard, you must seek approval. NEVER NEVER NEVER rely on the good will of the board or your neighbors when altering your property. For example, the president may be your friend and tell you it is fine to put up a shed. You don't need permission because it is under 120 sq feet, the county is fine with it, and the association is too. Five years later, a whole new board has taken over and they realize that your shed style doesn't match the community look. So they tell you that it must come down. Your friend died. And if you have to take it down, you lose a $6,000 investment.

Well-meaning folks might claim, “You're grandfathered in—the statute of limitations is up, so the board can't act.” In an association, though, if the documents don't explicitly allow any shed, you're out of luck. Without written permission from a prior board, new boards can pursue you. The risk? They can fine and penalize you until you comply—or you fight in court, where YOU CAN LOSE YOUR HOME. If you have permission in writing from the prior board, you have a 90% chance of winning in court. Even with permission, though, the board can change its mind and you are the one who gets fined!

Some states like Montana, have actually addressed this inequity. In Montana, a law was passed in 2025, saying if the covenant hasn't been enforced in two years, the HOA or Condo cannot enforce it (Mont. Code Ann. § 70-17-210). However, most states have left this in sort of a legal gray area called “laches” which refers to an equitable defense where a party's delay in enforcing a right (e.g., a covenant violation) can bar them from doing so later. Yet, relying on “laches” or “waiver by acquiescence” requires court battles and hefty legal fees.

Factoid: *Doris Vescio from Sun City Anthem in Nevada, faced $100 weekly fines for having a fence over the 6-foot limit. She installed it because a coyote had attacked and almost killed her Shih Tzu, Mitsi. Doris followed the process required by her HOA, got the stamps of approval from Architectural Committee but eight months later, she received a notice from her HOA that it had to come down. Within a short time she had accumulated over $7000 in fines.*

Always seek permission if it's not explicitly allowed in your documents— and save that permission document! The saying “It's better to beg for forgiveness than to ask for permission” doesn't hold in associations—don't be misled. Remember, your home is a major investment, and in an HOA, you don't truly own it. No handshake deal, however close the friendship, suffices. Protect yourself first.

Most associations and condominiums offer pre-made forms for handling requests and concerns, supplied by the board or management company. For smaller associations or when no form exists, AI can create one for you, in a fraction of the time that it would take on your own.

SPECIAL REQUESTS, APPROVALS, ALTERATIONS, WAIVERS

REQUEST FOR ALTERATIONS OR LANDSCAPING APPROVAL

Best Practices for Prompting Your AI to Request an Alteration to a Unit:

- Provide details on sizes, colors, and architectural style to clarify your plan.
- Attach pictures or a brochure when possible for visual reference.

- Include paint samples if available to aid decision-making.
- Request a response deadline (check if your documents specify a timeframe, after which approval may be assumed).

Request prompt to write a letter requesting Approval of Alteration to Unit_____
After your Master Prompt, add: "Draft a letter to the board of [*association name, e.g., Oak HOA*] in [*state, e.g., New Jersey*], requesting approval for an alteration to my home. I plan to install faux wooden shutters on all front windows, using earth tones in a clay slate color to match the western theme of the association. I will attach a brochure of the shutters. Please request a response by [*date, e.g., 09/01/2025*], and review association documents for relevant policies, citing them if applicable."

Request prompt to write a letter requesting Landscaping Approval
After your Master Prompt, add: "Draft a letter to the landscaping committee of *[association name, e.g., Oak HOA*] in [*state, e.g., New Jersey*], seeking approval to replace my lawn and flowers with xeriscaping. The city's new water restrictions concern me, as my lawn's decline could affect the community's appearance. I will attach a picture of the planned design. Please request a response by [*date, e.g., 09/01/2025*], and check association documents and the city's recent notice (online) for relevant citations."

Best Practices for Prompting Your AI to Design a Release Form from Your Neighbors:

- Ensure all adjoining neighbors sign a release to support your request, including it with your submission.
- Provide details and a picture or brochure so neighbors understand your proposed changes.
- Include this release even if not required by the association, as it can sway their decision. Request

Prompt for Designing a Release Form from Your Neighbors:
After your Master Prompt, add: "Draft a release form for [*association name, e.g., Oak HOA*] in [*state, e.g., New Jersey*], with space for six neighbor signatures, supporting the landscaping approval request drafted on [*date, e.g., 08/15/2025*]. My aim is to demonstrate to the association that my neighbors approve of my front yard xeriscaping plan."

SPECIAL NEEDS REQUESTS

The Federal Fair Housing Act (FHA) stands as one of the strongest laws supporting members seeking help from condominium or association boards. Its power lies in the ability to involve HUD for enforcement if your association denies a valid request—a rare law with real teeth in the HOA landscape. Qualifying for this can secure your needs without requiring an attorney to compel board compliance.

For disabilities affecting hearing, mobility, vision, alcoholism, mental illness, AIDS, or any major life activity, you can request reasonable accommodations for home access. This includes parking adjustments, snow removal, ramps, handrails, or upgrading rough gravel paths to smooth concrete walkways.

You might also be allowed to keep an animal under disability laws, even if covenants prohibit pets.

This covers guide dogs, seizure-alert dogs, comfort animals, and other service animals. You're not obligated to disclose your condition to the board, though you can. For a clear explanation of discrimination, check the Hindman Sanchez law firm's PDF, "Discrimination: An Overview of the Federal Fair Housing Act and a *Study of Discrimination Claims Filed Against Associations*" (available at www.altitude.law under Resources > Discrimination). It clarifies eligibility for accommodations or modifications and is quite helpful.

If the board delays or denies your accommodation, consider filing a complaint with HUD.

Best Practices for requesting an Accommodation Due to Disability

- Clearly describe the accommodation needed for your disability.
- Attach a letter from your healthcare provider, if available, to support your request.
- Direct your AI to research applicable state and federal Fair Housing Act codes for your disability, including relevant section quotes.
- Set a response deadline in your request.
- Add a sentence like: "If you are not the appropriate person to receive this request, please notify me immediately and forward this letter to the person handling reasonable accommodation requests."

Request Prompt for Accommodation Due to Disability:
After your Master Prompt, add: "Draft a request from me to the board of [*association name, e.g., Oak HOA*] in [*state, e.g., Mississippi*], for a wheelchair ramp at my front door, as I am now confined to a wheelchair with no other mobility option. Research state and federal Fair Housing Acts to identify mandates for associations to provide this accommodation, citing the relevant sections. Use the address from my Master Prompt for the unit in question. Request a response within 14 days of receipt, and include this sentence: 'If you are not the appropriate person to receive this request, please notify me immediately and forward this letter to the person handling reasonable accommodation requests.'"

SAMPLE OUTPUT (FROM GROK 3):

###

REQUEST FOR DISABILITY-RELATED ACCOMMODATION

FROM
[*Your Name*]
[*Street Address*]
[*City, State Zip*]
[*Phone*] [*Email*]

UNIT ADDRESS
[*123 Willow Rd, Lot 5*]
[*Grass Valley, UT 84029*]

TO
[*Willow HOA*]
[*456 Pine S*]
[*Grass Valley, UT 84029*]

DATE [*08/12/2025*]

Dear [*Secretary, President, or Manager*],

I am submitting a request for reasonable accommodation under the Federal Fair Housing Act (FHA) and the Utah Fair Housing Act. If you are not the appropriate person to receive this request, please notify me immediately and forward this letter to the person handling reasonable accommodation requests.

I have a disability covered by the FHA and Utah Fair Housing Act, specifically myasthenia gravis, which causes muscle weakness and breathing difficulties, requiring me to use a wheelchair. The stairs at my front entrance make it exhausting to access my unit. To address this, I need a ramp with a mild incline installed beside the stairs to allow my motorized wheelchair access to the first level, designed to blend with our community's aesthetic. The FHA (42 U.S.C. § 3604(f)(3)(A)) and Utah Code § 57-21-5(1)(a) mandate that associations provide such accommodations.

If you have alternative solutions, I'd welcome your suggestions to collaborate on a workable plan. I can provide medical documentation upon request. Please contact me at the above number or email if further information is needed, as my situation worsens daily without this support. I request a response within 14 days of receiving this letter.

Thank you,

[*Your Name*]

###

Factoid. The *Foundation for Community Association Research* reports that 25-27% of the U.S. population resides in private communities like condominiums, cooperatives, and housing associations. Additionally, federal laws mandate HOAs to provide disability accommodations, even if they conflict with governing documents.

MODIFICATION REQUEST TO UNIT DUE TO DISABILITY

There's a key difference between a request for accommodation and a modification. Typically, an accommodation seeks association-funded changes in common areas (within reason), while a modification involves alterations to your unit, paid for by you.

Prompt for a Modification Request to Unit Due to Disability

After your Master Prompt, add: "Draft a request from me to the board of [*association name, e.g., Oak HOA*] in [*state, e.g., Mississippi*], to replace the carpeting in my unit with beige travertine to ease wheelchair movement between rooms. Clarify that I will cover the cost. Have your AI research the Fair Housing Act (FHA) and Americans with Disabilities Act (ADA) to confirm mandates for such modifications, citing relevant sections. Use the address from my Master Prompt for the unit. Request a response within 14 days of receipt, including this sentence: 'If you are not the appropriate person to receive this request, please notify me immediately and forward this letter to the person handling reasonable accommodation requests.'"

Factoid: *In 2015 an HOA sent a letter to a pastor who had suffered a stroke which read, "The association demands that within 14 days of the date of this letter, you remove the wheelchair ramp and restore the exterior of your home." The Broadnax's originally described it as "insensitive" and wondered how to comply AND make the home accessible to the disabled husband. The letter was* *harsh, insensitive, and stupid. Fortunately someone on the board got wise to the Americans with Disabilities Act and the Federal Housing Act and backtracked saying, "The board did not know the ramp was for the homeowner, Mr. Broadnax. The association would like to work with the owners on a compromise..." Really? Then why was the letter addressed to them? Ask yourself why no one on the board, the attorney or the manager knew about the Americans with Disabilities Act.*

WAIVERS

Do not confuse a "Request for Waiver of Fees" with a "Dispute Request" or "Hearing Request." A dispute or hearing challenges a violation you didn't commit or argue it shouldn't apply, while a waiver admits the act but claims you're not at fault—e.g., your dog pooped, but you rushed for a baggie. If unsure which fits, opt for a waiver. Why? It's non-confrontational, framing it as a favor, which is less likely to ruffle management or Trustee feathers.

Best Practices for Prompting Your AI to Request a Waiver of Fees:

- Submit all waiver requests for fines, rules, late charges, or assessments in writing.
- Clearly outline the circumstances and justification, e.g., "My payment was late due to a holiday weekend for International Day of the Rodent in Cove's Creek—I didn't know the office was closed.
- With a strong payment history, I request a waiver of the one-day late fee."
- Specify the exact fee or penalty (e.g., late fees, interest, fines, repair charges) and the amount sought.
- Avoid withholding payment past the deadline—pay first, then request the waiver. Submit before the due date to delay payment without penalties; if granted, request reimbursement.

Prompt for Requesting a Waiver of Fees

After your Master Prompt, add: "Draft a letter addressed to the secretary of [*association name, e.g., Double Trouble HOA*] in [*state, e.g., New Mexico*], requesting a correction for a payment issue. Explain that I received a notice for a $129 fine and repair cost for my mailbox, which I believe is incorrect since the HOA snowplow damaged it on [*date, e.g., 01/15/2025*], and the driver assured me it would be covered. I paid the $129 to avoid penalties and now seek a refund, suggest this was an *inadvertent oversight*. Review association documents for relevant payment policies and cite them if applicable."

Best Practices for Prompting AI to Request a Waiver of Rules:

- This is a waiver of some rule or policy from which you want to be exempted, such as for special dates like grand-kids visiting on Easter or pool hours.
- Mention and cite it, if you believe the regulation is not in compliance with federal or state law and want a waiver until the board resolves it. Your board may be unaware of any violation. Have AI research the law first so you can cite it.
- Give exact dates fro which you want the waiver.

Prompt for Requesting a Waiver of Rules

After your Master Prompt, add: "Draft a polite letter to the secretary of *[association name, e.g., Double Trouble HOA*] in [state, e.g., California], requesting a waiver of the rule designating 'adults-only' pool hours after 5 PM. Explain that my nieces and nephews, visiting from August 7 to August 10, 2025, attend day camp and can only swim in the evening. Emphasize my commitment to HOA rules but note that 'adults-only' restrictions may violate the federal Fair Housing Act's familial status protections, as seen in *Landesman v. The Keys Condominium Owners Association* (2004, California), where a court ruled that excluding children from a main pool during certain hours was discriminatory. Request a waiver for those dates, ask for confirmation, and sign with 'Sincerely.' Format for formal submission."

Note if the board denies your waiver request: If the board denies your waiver, prompt your AI for a deep search of these agencies to check for relevant policies or protections, ensuring compliance with laws tied to your request:

- Americans with Disabilities Act
- Environmental Protection Agency Complaints
- Fair Debt Collection
- Fair Housing Act (HUD has protected classes which you may be a member of)
- California Fair Housing Act (expands HUD's protected classes)
- Fair Labor Standards Act
- Freedom to Display the American Flag Act
- Servicemembers Civil Relief Act (SCRA)
- The United States Bankruptcy Code
- Over-the-Air Reception Devices Rule (OTARD)

Common non-compliance examples include "Adult Swim Time" rules (discriminatory unless for 55+ communities), FCC bans on prohibiting satellite dishes, and "right to dry" laws in states like Arizona, California, Colorado, Florida, Hawaii, Illinois, Indiana, Louisiana, Maine, Maryland, Massachusetts, Nevada, New Mexico, North Carolina, Oregon, Texas, Utah, Vermont, Virginia, and Wisconsin, allowing clotheslines.

If your community is spraying chemicals for weed control, and you believe they are toxic, request a waiver from spraying. Read the label carefully. Many of these chemicals are to be used *as stated* on the label or it is a violation of EPA regulations, a federal offense. Weed sprays are governed by the EPA--so your waiver request may well save your association from a law suit, depending on what chemical is used. Again, let your AI advocate do a deep research on the subject, and make recommendations about your options.

Most waivers involve minor issues (e.g., planting daisies over chrysanthemums for color harmony or using laundry off-hours for work). Include a neighbor release form (see "REQUEST FOR APPROVAL FOR ALTERATIONS OR LANDSCAPING") if needed. If the association breaks laws, start with a non-confrontational waiver request, suggesting they review your evidence. If they resist pettily, escalate to the proper agency—Trustees might regret ignoring you.

PARKING VARIANCE REQUEST

Parking rules are a persistent headache in associations. I get why some focus on them—no one wants a yard full of cars on blocks. Many residents might initially support these rules, but they often spiral out of control. I recall trying to buy a small trailer from a man in a southern California HOA—a tidy double-wide trailer suburb, hardly upscale. I parked in front, chatted for about 10 minutes, then hitched the trailer for a test drive, totaling under 30 minutes. A week later, I returned. He rushed out, urging me into his carport, and over his kitchen table, showed me a warning letter from the board. Cars aren't allowed on the street at all! A neighbor snapped a photo of my visit and reported him for my 15-minute stay. In a trailer court, no less! What drives people to police streets and neighbors like that?

Best Practices for Prompting Your AI to Request a Parking Variance:

- Clearly state the parking location and the vehicle's owner.
- Include a vehicle description and license plate number for identification
- Specify the variance dates, from start to end.
- For a permanent variance, suggest a small "rent" payment to assure the board it's not an unfair request.

Request Prompt for a Parking Variance:
After your Association Master Prompt, add: "Draft a request to the board of [*association name, e.g., Oak HOA*] in [*state, e.g., New Jersey*], citing our applicable state code, for a parking variance during spring break. Explain that my son, visiting from college, needs parking since our garage is full, requesting permission for his RAV4 in the driveway from April 18 to April 23, 2025. Specify that I'll submit this via the board's online portal by email."

RENTAL
Many associations require one to seek permission to rent a unit or home, especially in condominiums. If the bylaws require permission to rent your home or unit then the board or management company will have forms for an application. If not, they may just require the gathering of information for safety reasons. Even without a requirement, notifying the board or management by *registered letter* when renting is a wise precaution.

Best Practices for Prompting Your AI to Provide Tenant Information to an Association Board:

- After board approval, submit tenant information as soon as they move in.
- Include a lease clause confirming tenants have read and agreed to follow the association's rules and regulations.
- Make sure to include the description and license plates of the tenant's vehicles.
- Make sure management can contact you should the renters violate the documents.
- Pay violations promptly, even if your renters contest it, so you don't build up penalties, then take up the issue with renters later.

Request Prompt for Providing Notification to the Board with Tenant Information:
After your Master Prompt, add: "Draft a notification letter to the board, addressed to the secretary of [*association name, e.g., Oak HOA*] in [*state, e.g., New Jersey*], informing them of a new tenant at [*456 Pine Tree Ln*]. Include the tenant names [*e.g., Jane Doe, John Doe, Child Doe*], phone number [*e.g., 555-123-4567*], and details of their two vehicles *[e.g., Blue Sedan, License ABC123; Red SUV, License XYZ789*]. Specify that assessments and violation notices should be sent to me for immediate handling. Attach a lease copy, noting tenants have read and intend to follow the CC&Rs and Rules and Regulations. Conclude by asking if further information is needed, providing my current address, email [*e.g., member@oakhoa.org*], and phone [*e.g., 555-987-6543*] for contact."

RIGHTS TO RECORDS

Homeowners have long enjoyed the right to inspect and copy association records under most corporate codes and sound business practices. Yet, this right offers no guarantees. Accessing records, especially financial ones, often proves challenging, with Trustees sometimes acting as gatekeepers, treating requests as personal attacks.

Most states have passed laws explicitly granting association members access to the records of the organization they support. Across the country, corporate codes affirm shareholders' rights to inspect and copy, but boards frequently ignore or block these requests. Despite these laws, enforcement is lacking, leaving record access a gamble—will the board comply or react defensively?

Jan Bergemann writes about HOA record requests in Florida and calls them "Statutes Without Teeth."

> *There is absolutely no way to enforce the requirements of these statutes without going to court – after going to pre-suit mediation – and wasting a lot of time and money. An owner facing a stubborn board/CAM is out more than $500 before seeing a judge in small claims court and asking for the $500 penalty allowed by statute for "damages for the association's willful failure to comply with the record-inspection requirements".*
>
> *We have even seen cases where judges granted the owner the $500 penalty, but couldn't force the association to give the owner access to the demanded records. What a joke!*

Unfortunately, not the kind of joke one laughs at.

> **Factoid:** *In 2012, records and transparency issues accounted for about 17 percent of complaints coming into Colorado's newly formed HOA Information Office and Resource Center. A lack of transparency makes it harder for homeowners to know whether associations are doing their job.*
>
> **Factoid:** *In Hawaii, the State Licensing Board is adamant that condominium owners have access to records and they accept complaints when an owner is refused access to association documents. They even provide a detailed form online. It is an ideal that other states should emulate—however, this excellent homeowner protection only applies to condominiums and not HOAs.*

Best Practices for Prompting Your AI to Make a Records Request in Your HOA or Condominium:

- Start with an informal email to the Secretary; if unsuccessful, draft a letter stating your purpose briefly.
- Specify the exact documents (e.g., financial overview, member lists for a board campaign, board resolutions) and their purpose.
- Avoid vague requests like "I want all the records."
- Define the date range for the records sought.
- Indicate your preferred delivery method: email, paper copies (noting possible charges), or in-person inspection.
- Send the request via registered letter or deliver in person with a receipt.

Request Prompt for Records Request:
After your Master Prompt, add: "Draft a Records Request letter to the Secretary of [*association name, e.g., Oak HOA*] in [*state, e.g., New Jersey*], requesting the contact information for all association members to support my board campaign. Have your AI review our applicable state code and CC&Rs to confirm my right to these records, citing relevant sections. Specify a delivery deadline of [*date, e.g., 09/01/2025*] to align with my campaign launch."

INSURANCE POLICY

You may request copies of the association's insurance policy to confirm coverage and identify contacts if the board acts improperly. Writing to the association attorney often falls flat, as they typically align with the board's agenda. In contrast, involving an insurance company, with a financial stake in what the association does, might yield results.

Requesting these policies could also secure little extra protection for you. Sara Benson, in "Escaping Condo Jail," shares a clever tactic I hadn't considered: "If a board is hoarding information and proper demand has been made for documents, one powerful tool is to copy both the association's attorney and the association's insurance carrier—via Certified US Mail—advising them of the improper board behavior. If they investigate and find that an association's directors are acting improperly, they can address the impropriety or choose to terminate their services. Further, the association may be at risk of losing insurance coverage. Directors' and officers' insurance won't cover them if they break the law. The insurance carrier will wonder: If they are ignoring state statutes what other issues are they ignoring?" ~Benson, Sara E.; DeBat, Don (2014-11-05). *Escaping Condo Jail*

Request Prompt for a copy of the Association Insurance Policy:
After your Master Prompt, add: "Draft a Records Request letter to the Secretary of [*association name, e.g., Oak HOA*] in [*state, e.g., New Jersey*], I would like to see the insurance policy we have for our association so I know what coverage I may need in addition to our general policy and assure myself we are adequately covered here. Please cite our state's Common Interest Development Act and CC&Rs where it gives me the right to these records. I can receive therecords either by mail or email."

PAYOFF REQUESTS

When selling a property within an HOA, obtaining a clear payoff statement for assessments is critical, especially as some states have enacted laws to protect buyers. For example, in Utah, HOAs must register with the state and keep contact information current so real estate agents or title companies can easily access payoff details. If an HOA fails to update its registration, it cannot enforce a lien on the property. However, enforcement of such laws often requires costly court action. Even if an HOA improperly places a lien, counties may still refuse to record a new title without a lien release, rendering such laws ineffective without proactive measures.

Best Practices for Prompting Your AI to Request an Assessment Payoff

- Instruct your AI to draft a written payoff statement request detailing all monies owed.
- Confirm the date through which the payoff amount is valid.
- Ensure your AI specifies that the statement includes assessments, fines, penalties, and late fees, representing the total amount owed.
- If working with a title company or real estate agent, allow them to handle the request, as they are experienced in obtaining accurate payoff information.

Prompt Request for an Assessment Payoff
After your Master Prompt, add: "Draft a professional letter to the treasurer of [*association name, e.g., Oak HOA*] in [*state, e.g., New Jersey*], requesting a complete payoff statement for all assessments, fines, penalties, and late fees owed on [*e.g., 456 Pine Tree Ln*]. Include a request for the date through which the payoff amount is valid. Use a polite yet firm tone, and ensure the letter is formatted for formal correspondence."

GENERAL REQUESTS

PET PEEVES

Most HOAs and property associations permit pets with restrictions, while many condominiums enforce strict policies on pet weight, number, or species, or prohibit pets entirely. If pets are allowed, check if registration is required. Even if not mandatory, submitting a Notice of Pet Ownership is wise. Notifying the board establishes a record, which can grandfather your pet if the HOA later adopts a "no pets" policy—a common occurrence. Submitting the notice at a board meeting ensures it's recorded in the minutes as a permanent record. The form below is designed for members to submit to the board but can be adapted by AI for use as an official HOA form.

Factoid: California is the only state explicitly granting owners the right to keep one pet, *"No governing documents (including operating rules) passed or amended after January 1, 2010 may prohibit an owner from keeping one pet, subject to reasonable rules and regulations of the association." (Civil Code Section 4715).* Because of this law, owners don't have to pretend their animal is a service pet in order to keep one. But that is another issue.

Best Practices for Submitting a Notification of Pet Ownership

- Submit a Notice of Pet Ownership, even if not required, to protect your rights.
- Include the pet's breed, weight, sex, spay/neuter status, and distinguishing marks.
- Provide proof of licensing, vaccinations, or a veterinarian's health certification, if applicable.
- Use your AI to confirm the HOA's pet policy and tailor the notice to comply with specific requirements.

Request Prompt to create a Notification of Pet Ownership:
After your Master Prompt, add: "Draft a Notice to the Secretary of [*association name, e.g., Oak HOA*] in [*state, e.g., New Jersey*], informing them that I have a pet, I have a 3 year old female mini

Aussie, 21 pounds, spayed, with blue eyes. Her shots are up to date and I will provide the records if requested." I will only walk her on a leash and will clean up any messes that occur. Ask if they more than this notification and sign with "Kind regards."

###

NOTICE OF PET OWNERSHIP

FROM
[Pet Owners Name]
I am a ___Tenant ___Owner
[Phone] [Email]

UNIT ADDRESS
[Street Address]
[City, State Zip]

TO
[Legal Name of Association]
[Street Address of Association]
[City, State Zip]

______________________ Kind of Pet ______________ Breed ______________ Pet answers to "Name"

____________ Pet's Age ____________ Pet's Weight (dogs only) ______________________ Distinguishing marks

_________Male _________Female _________Fixed _________Not fixed

Proof of license and rabies shots is attached. [*Or for pets other than dogs, a certification of good health from a veterinarian*]

A photo of my pride and joy is also attached.

I have read the Association's pet policy and my family agrees to abide by the rules. I understand that if my pet causes a problem that I will take care of it once noticed by the neighbors or management. I also understand that it is my responsibility to see that I am insured for liability and release the association from any liability claims should someone make a claim as a result of my pet. I am fully responsible for any and all claims for injury or other damages caused by my pet.

______________________________ Signature of Pet Owner ____________ Date

______________________________ Signature and title of Association representative ____________ Date

###

SERVICE ANIMAL
Under the Americans with Disabilities Act (ADA), a service animal is a dog trained to perform specific

tasks to assist individuals with disabilities in work or public spaces. Emotional support animals may not qualify under the ADA but can be considered "assistance animals" (also called "companion animals") under the Fair Housing Act (FHA) or Section 504 of the Rehabilitation Act. These animals, which don't need to be dogs or formally trained, may provide psychiatric support for conditions like depression, claustrophobia, autism, high blood pressure, or PTSD. While HOAs cannot ask about your disability, they may require proof (e.g., a medical report from a physician or psychiatrist) to verify the need for an assistance animal.

Best Practices for Prompting Your AI to Notify an HOA of a Service or Assistance Animal

- Instruct your AI to draft a notice specifying whether the animal is a service animal (ADA) or assistance animal (FHA/Section 504). Generally, you will use the FHA to justify keeping a pet. Ask AI to cite relevant laws to strengthen the notice.
- Always include the breed, weight, and distinguishing marks on your pet.
- Give the sex and information on whether your pet is spayed.
- Ask if any further information or documentation is needed.

Request Prompt for Notification of Retaining an Assistance Animal:

After your Master Prompt, add: "Draft a formal notice to the secretary of [*association name, e.g., Oak HOA*] in [*state, e.g., New Jersey*], stating that I am retaining an assistance animal under the Fair Housing Act (FHA) or Section 504, a 3-year-old spayed Tabby cat with up-to-date vaccinations (records available upon request). Note that she is an indoor cat. Ask if further documentation is required and sign with 'Kind regards.' Format the notice for submission at a board meeting."

EVENT PERMISSION REQUEST

Many HOAs, especially gated communities, require permission to post signs or host events like yard sales, block parties, or holiday picnics. Some communities, like Grass Valley's Property Owners Association, lack clear rules due to board turnover or petty disputes, leading to inconsistent enforcement. People here are free to put up signs along the roads any time they want, unless a board member decides on his or her own that they can't! We had two bully board members who were seen driving along and pulling down the signs leading to a girl's sweet 16 birthday party! Honestly, some of our Members here in Grass Valley are incredibly petty. Naturally, it was the daughter of Diane, a Member whom they had labeled a "troublemaker." Not surprisingly, Diane is now on the board! This highlights the need for clear requests to avoid conflicts. Proactive communication can also build goodwill, as today's targeted member may become tomorrow's board leader.

Best Practices for Prompting Your AI to Request Permission for an Event

- Instruct your AI to draft a request specifying the event type, date, time, and location.
- Direct your AI to research the HOA's CC&Rs to confirm compliance with event or signage rules.

- Note any temporary signs, their placement, and removal plan.
- Ask your AI to address parking needs for guests and ensure the request is polite but firm.

Request Prompt for Requesting Permission for a Yard Sale (*customize to event*):
After your Master Prompt, add: "Draft a formal letter to the board of [*association name, e.g., Magical Mountain HOA*] in [*state, e.g., Arkansas*], requesting permission for a yard sale on Saturday, May 9, from 9 AM to 5 PM, hosted by three neighbors. Note that we will place four directional signs along community streets, to be removed by 6 PM. Confirm compliance with the HOA's CC&Rs and ask if additional details are needed. Use a courteous tone and sign with 'Sincerely.'"

CONSENT FOR ELECTRONIC RECEIPT OF RECORDS, NOTIFICATIONS, AND ASSESSMENTS

Many HOAs offer electronic delivery of newsletters, notices, and assessments, often requested via an Owner Information form (see Chapter Eight: Communications). If your form lacks this option, a simple AI-drafted email or letter can suffice. Note that legal documents like lien notices, foreclosure notices, or attorney letters typically require physical delivery due to legal requirements.

Best Practices for Prompting Your AI to Request Electronic Receipt of Records

- Instruct your AI to draft a concise request specifying the types of documents (e.g., newsletters, assessments) and your preferred email.
- Confirm the HOA's process for electronic delivery and ask for acknowledgment.
- Have your AI note that legal documents (e.g., liens) are expected via physical mail, per standard practice.

Prompt for Consent for Electronic Receipt of Records and Documents
After your Master Prompt, add: "Draft a concise email to the secretary of [*association name, e.g., Oak HOA*] in [*state, e.g., New Jersey*], requesting electronic delivery of association documents, such as newsletters, notices, and assessments, to [*email, e.g., Johndoe@gmail.com*]. Ask for confirmation of receipt and the process for electronic delivery. Note that I understand legal documents may require physical mail. Sign with 'Best regards.'"

CLEAN-UP/MAINTENANCE REQUESTS

Requests for clean-up, repairs, or services (e.g., clubhouse air-conditioning or winter walk salting) should be concise and professional. Start with a positive tone, such as acknowledging the board's efforts, to foster cooperation. Avoid citing HOA covenants or bylaws initially unless the issue persists beyond two weeks, at which point referencing specific documents can strengthen your request. Always copy the board when contacting management.

Best Practices for Prompting Your AI to Request a Clean-Up in the Common Area

- Instruct your AI to specify the exact location and nature of the clean-up needed.
- Avoid vague language (e.g., "clean the place up").
- Attach photos, if available, to clarify the issue.
- Ask AI to include a polite acknowledgment of the board's efforts and cc the board secretary.

Prompt for Requesting a Clean-Up in the Common Area
After your Master Prompt, add: "Draft an email to the management company of [*association name,*

e.g., Oak HOA] in [*state, e.g., New Jersey*], requesting clean-up of the dumpster area behind the retaining pond, where garbage has been scattered by a bear for over two weeks. Note that I am attaching a photo and show some appreciation for the board's maintenance efforts. Cc the association secretary and sign with 'Best regards.'"

Best Practices for Prompting Your AI to Request a Repair in the Common Area

- Instruct your AI to describe the repair needed in detail, including any safety hazards.
- Attach photos, if possible, to illustrate the issue.
- Include a polite acknowledgment of the board's work and cc the board secretary.
- Ask your AI to confirm the correct recipient or request forwarding to the appropriate party.

AI Prompt to Request a Repair in the Common Area

After your Master Prompt, add: "Draft an email to the management company of [association name, e.g., Oak HOA] in [state, e.g., New Jersey], requesting repair of a broken bench in the community park, which poses a safety hazard due to exposed nails. Note that I'm attaching a photo and express appreciation for the board's upkeep efforts. Cc the association secretary and ask if this is the correct contact. Sign with 'Best regards.'"

Best Practices for Prompting Your AI to Request a Service in the Common Area

- Instruct your AI to describe the expected service (e.g., holiday decorations) with specific details and timelines.
- Have AI research the HOA's governing documents to identify the responsible party (e.g., committee or management).
- Ask if the correct contact was reached and request forwarding if needed.
- Ask your AI to maintain a courteous tone to encourage cooperation.

AI Prompt to request a Service in the Common Area

After your Master Prompt, add: "Draft an email to the management company of [*association name, e.g., Oak HOA*] in [*state, e.g., New Jersey*], asking if Christmas decorations will be installed in the community room before the members' Christmas dinner on December 16 to ensure a festive atmosphere. Confirm if this is the correct contact or request forwarding to the responsible committee. Sign with 'Best regards.'"

CONFRONTING BULLY BOARDS & RESPONDING TO VIOLATIONS

Bully boards cost HOA communities millions annually in lawsuits and disputes. Board members often label advocate members as "troublemakers," deflecting blame for conflicts, though some members, like Horace with his 75 dogs, do cause issues. Most homeowners avoid court due to time and cost, but unchecked bully boards—ignoring governing documents, enforcing rules haphazardly, or acting with impunity—push rational owners to their limits. Thus boards often do anything they want, without reading or following the documents (leaving it up to the industry "experts"), can be completely arbitrary and capricious about enforcement with little oversight, including members of the association who want to "forgive and forget." When called on the carpet, bully boards remind the Members that they are just "volunteers."

Unfortunately, Members must be more than diligent in dealing with boards, who can go "bully" at a moment's notice. Even if you follow all the rules, you should keep records of your compliance. Keep all bank statements, proof of payment for assessments, receipts for amenities, and proof of correction of violations. If you were grandfathered in for something with one board, keep that in writing. Never assume the next board will honor what the last board did unless you have proof. Consider recording the more important variances you receive at the county clerk's office.

For instance. Grass Valley is primarily a recreational subdivision. Many Members put up single wide trailers, turning them into little "cabins" for weekend use. Twenty years ago they were given waivers allowing them to be used as permanent structures as long as they didn't reside there. Recently, a few new Trustees expressed their distaste for "drag-ins" and began turning these owners into the county officials. The "drag-in" owners had relied on the good will of past Trustees never considering their small close-knit community would someday be infiltrated with self-centered Members turned into Bully Boards.

To safeguard your rights:

- Retain written proof of variances or waivers.
- Record significant variances at the county clerk's office.
- Document all interactions with the board, including emails and meeting minutes.

Some states offer resources to combat HOA abuses:

- Nevada: The Real Estate Division's CIC Manual (https://red.nv.gov/uploadedFiles/rednvgov/Content/CIC/Manual/CIC_Manual.pdf) outlines homeowner rights and responsibilities.
- Virginia: The Common Interest Community Ombudsman (CICO) provides a formal complaint process with a flowchart explaining steps. Associations must have an internal complaint policy and share ombudsman contact details, with fines up to $1,000 per violation for non-compliance.
- California: The Center for California Homeowner Association Law was set up by Marjorie Murray (calhomelaw.org/) with the help of some grants just for the purposes of lobbying for HOA law and protecting consumers. California offers robust HOA protections, including mediation and arbitration options.
- Arizona: The Department of Real Estate (ADRE) offers dispute resolution through an Administrative Law Judge for $500, though this process may soon be repealed, forcing homeowners back to costly civil courts.
- Delaware: After hearing about massive HOA & Condo frustrations and abuses, the Delaware State Legislature in 2018 assigned a point-person to help handle such conflicts. A Common Interest Community Ombudsperson now assists with complaints and provides a downloadable dispute form: Ombudsman's Template Internal Dispute Rules.

Quote *Legislation without effective enforcement through monetary penalties is merely a recommendation that relies on the good faith of the parties, namely the board and its attorney and* *manager advisors. But, we know all about the good faith acts of many of these responsible parties, especially those of rogue boards that ignore the laws and governing documents or knowingly violate them with impunity.* ~George K. Staropoli, HOA Constitutional Rights Attorney

VIOLATIONS

When dealing with violations, please do not ignore them because they are "silly" or "stupid." Boards can legally pursue minor infractions, like unmowed lawns or unapproved blinds, leading to hefty fines or even foreclosure.

Factoid: *David Moore, a San Antonio resident, is being sued by his board for hundreds of thousands of dollars in ridiculous violations like not cutting his grass enough, a 17-year-old cat door in his garage, and incorrect blinds on his windows. He ignored the warnings he considered "ridiculous" and now it really has gotten ridiculous. It amounts to over $200,000. Trying to warn his neighbors, Moore put up a large sign in his front yard, "the HOA has spent $50,000 in attorney fees fighting me for violations." Guess what the next warning letter will be about?*

Best Practices for Prompting Your AI to Address Bully Boards or Violations

- Instruct your AI to draft a response to violation notices, citing specific compliance actions or requesting clarification.
- Direct your AI to research state agencies (e.g., ombudsmen or real estate departments) and their complaint processes.
- Have your AI identify key contacts in relevant government departments for support.
- Ask your AI to review your HOA's governing documents to ensure the board's actions align with rules.
- Request a professional, non-confrontational tone to avoid escalating disputes.

Prompt for Responding to a Violation Notice

After your Master Prompt, add: "Draft a formal letter to the board of [*association name, e.g., Oak HOA*] in [*state, e.g., New Jersey*], responding to a violation notice dated [date] regarding [issue, e.g., unapproved fence]. State that I have corrected the issue by [*action, e.g., removing the fence*] and attach proof (*e.g., photos*). Request confirmation of compliance and ask if further action is needed. Research the HOA's CC&Rs to ensure the violation aligns with governing documents. Use a polite, professional tone and sign with 'Sincerely.'"

Prompt for Researching State Resources for HOA Disputes

After your Master Prompt, add: "Conduct a DeepSearch for state-specific resources in [state, e.g., Virginia] to address HOA disputes, such as ombudsmen, real estate departments, or mediation programs. Provide a list of agencies, contact details, and complaint processes. Draft a brief email to [*agency, e.g., Virginia CICO*] inquiring about support for a dispute with [*association name, e.g., Oak HOA*] regarding [*issue, e.g., arbitrary violation enforcement*]. Sign with 'Best regards.'"

COMPLAINT FORMS

Filing complaints against neighbors is basically "snitching" on them and often escalates conflicts. They should used only as a last resort. While some issues, like persistent disturbances, may warrant action, direct communication is usually better than reporting to the HOA board. In the first edition of HOA Warrior, a neighbor complaint form was included, but it's been removed from this edition to avoid fueling disputes like the "War of the Roses" (see factoid). Instead, focus on resolving issues amicably with neighbors (e.g., over barking dogs or yard debris) using AI to draft polite letters. Vendor complaints, however, are different and may require formal action if the board or management fails to address unprofessional behavior.

Factoid: *A Rancho Santa Fe, California, HOA targeted Jeffery DeMarco for planting too many rose bushes on his four-acre property. When DeMarco balked, the HOA levied monthly fines, threatened foreclosure, and ultimately defeated DeMarco in court. After a judge ruled that the willful rose enthusiast had violated the community's architecture design rules, DeMarco was forced to pay the HOA's $70,000 legal bill and lost his home to the bank.*

Best Practices for Prompting Your AI to Address Neighbor Issues Amicably

- Instruct your AI to draft a polite, non-confrontational letter to your neighbor describing the issue (e.g., barking dog) and proposing a solution.
- Have AI research your HOA's CC&Rs to ensure your request aligns with community rules.
- Suggest mediation options if direct communication fails, avoiding formal complaints.

Prompt for Addressing a Neighbor Issue

After your Master Prompt, add: "Draft a polite letter to my neighbor at [*address, e.g., 123 Oak St., Springfield, NJ*], explaining that their dog's barking after 10 PM is disturbing my family's sleep. Suggest a meeting to discuss solutions, such as keeping the dog indoors at night. Research the [*association name, e.g., Oak HOA*] CC&Rs to confirm noise rules and include a relevant reference if applicable. Sign with 'Kind regards' and format for friendly communication.

Best Practices for Complaining about Vendor Behavior or Work

- When complaining about a vendor, frame the complaint as a "request for investigation" about the vendors behavior to avoid being labeled a troublemaker. This encourages the board to see themselves as helping you. It's a matter of perception.
- Always include the date, time, and name of the vendor if you have it.
- Describe their behavior as best you can.
- Include evidence [e.g. a witness, photo, suggest reviewing security camera].
- If it is something of a sexual nature such as a vendor peeking inside your window, or making a pass at you, or touching you inappropriately, consider reporting it to the police rather than your HOA. It's a judgment call.

Prompt Request for Writing a Letter of Complaint Regarding a Vendor:

After your Master Prompt, add: "Draft a non-confrontational letter to the president of [*association name, e.g., Oak HOA*] in [*state, e.g., New Jersey*], requesting investigation of an incident on [date and time, e.g., July 10, 2025, at 2 PM] involving XYZ Fence Company. While repairing a gate latch, an unnamed worker kicked my 4-pound dog, Mitzi, who was barking but not nipping, as witnessed by [neighbor name]. Note that Mitzi appears uninjured but request they provide advance notice of future repairs to prevent a recurrence. Sign with 'Sincerely' and format for formal submission to the board with a cc to the management company."

Note if the board ignores your investigation request: In the event that you get no satisfaction from your board (since they hired the manager or landscaper or attorney, they may not be inclined to listen to you) you can escalate the complaint to the next level:

- Better Business Bureau

- Fair Housing Act (filing a complaint for discrimination)
- Consumer Protection
- Attorney General (in your state)
- State Bar (If this about your association attorney)
- Real Estate Board (If managers are regulated by the real estate board in your state)
- CAI (If your manager is CAI certified in your state, use this form)
- Florida Complaint Package against Managers (some states, like Florida have complaint forms online

Best Practices for Prompting Your AI to Escalate a Vendor Complaint

- Instruct AI to research state-specific agencies (e.g., DCA in New Jersey) and their complaint processes.
- Have AI to draft a complaint letter citing evidence and desired outcomes (e.g., vendor retraining).
- Have your AI identify the correct agency contact and confirm submission requirements.
- Maintain a professional tone to maximize the complaint's impact.

Prompt for Escalating a Vendor Complaint to an External Agency

After your Master Prompt, add: "Conduct a DeepSearch for the best agency in [*state, e.g., New Jersey*] to handle a complaint against a vendor hired by [*association name, e.g., Oak HOA]* for [*issue, e.g., unprofessional behavior on July 10, 2025*]. Draft a complaint letter to the [agency, e.g., New Jersey Department of Community Affairs], detailing the incident with XYZ Fence Company kicking my dog, including [*evidence, e.g., witness statement, photo*]. Request investigation and vendor accountability. Confirm submission requirements and sign with 'Best regards.'"

CONTESTING OR DISPUTING BOARD ACTIONS

Receiving a warning or notice for violating an HOA covenant or rule requires immediate action. If you committed the violation, correct it promptly to avoid escalation—small infractions can lead to significant fines or even foreclosure, as outlined earlier in this book. No one is exempt, so don't assume leniency. Boards often face criticism from irate members, so frame your response as a request for assistance rather than a confrontation. Admitting a violation (if true) with an explanation—similar to a "no contest" plea in court—makes boards more receptive. Avoid inflammatory openings like, "*This is the dumbest rule ever,*" which can alienate trustees and taint their view of your case. If you believe the warning is incorrect, dispute it carefully with evidence and a professional and even friendly tone. Remember, they are your neighbors. Whether addressing a violation, late payment notice, or fine, politeness and documentation are key to resolving disputes without escalating tensions.

NO matter how stupid you think the rules or regulations are or how petty you think they are for warning you, take the higher road. Do let them know that you intend to comply. Apologize. Be happy that you dodged a bullet. Be nice--be lighthearted--and hope they like you. On the other hand, if you did not commit the act, use caution in protesting. Here are some guidelines.

Best Practices for Prompting Your AI to Dispute a Warning or Fine

- Instruct your AI to draft a brief, unemotional letter explaining why the warning or fine is incorrect (e.g., mistaken identity, compliance with bylaws, or a change in state law).
- Direct your AI to cite specific bylaws, CC&Rs, or state laws to support your case.

- Avoid personal attacks, even if the complaint feels petty or unfair.
- If you technically violated a rule but believe it's unfairly enforced (e.g., others violate similarly), ask your AI to request equal enforcement politely.
- Include evidence (e.g., photos, bank statements) to strengthen your dispute.

Request Prompt to Dispute a Warning Notice
After your Master Prompt, add: "Draft a letter disputing a warning I was given from [*association name, e.g., Oak HOA*] in [*state, e.g., New Jersey*], I was accused of not having my trash can in by 5PM every week. This is true. I usually get it in after work by around 8PM, sometimes later, but I always return my trash can on trash day. I read the bylaws and they say our trash cans have to be "in by the end of the day." Technically that is 11:59PM. Cite the bylaw and explain that I am following the bylaws and would like the warning expunged from my records. I want the letter to sound accommodating."

Request Prompt to Appeal a Fine
After your Master Prompt, add: "Draft a letter disputing a fine I was given from the management company of [*association name, e.g., Oak HOA*] in [*state, e.g., New Jersey*]. I was accused of not having my trash can in by 5PM every week. This is true. I usually get it in after work by around 8PM, sometimes later, but I always return my trash can on trash day. I read the bylaws and they say our trash cans have to be "in by the end of the day." Technically that is 11:59PM. Cite the bylaw and explain that I am following the bylaws and would appreciate them dropping the fine. Refer to the letter of explanation I already sent after receiving the warning. Ask if I should request a hearing before the board to clarify the issue. Address the letter to the president of the association with a cc to the management company. I want the letter to sound friendly."

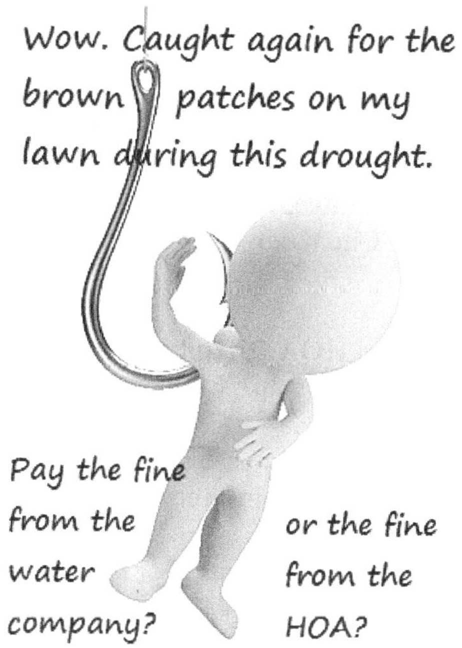

Best Practice for Requesting a Correction Regarding a Late Payment Notice.

- Instruct your AI to draft a polite letter avoiding blame or terms like "mistake" (use "inadvertent oversight" or "omission" instead).
- Have your AI request confirmation of correction and express appreciation for the board's efforts.
- Always include evidence. (Screen shots of payments, deposit slips, credit card statements..etc)
- Upload the notification letter to your AI so it has all the particulars.

Request Prompt to Request a Correction in Payment
After your Master Prompt, add: "Draft a polite email to the bookkeeper of [*association name, e.g., Oak HOA*] in [*state, e.g., New Jersey*], explaining that I sent a check on [*date, e.g. 6/5/2024*], cashed a week later before the due date, per my attached bank statement. Request correction of the payment record due to an inadvertent oversight. Express appreciation for the bookkeeper's efforts and sign with 'Best regards.'"

HEARING

"Holding an HOA disciplinary hearing is common practice among many homeowners associations when a violation has occurred. Both the HOA board and homeowners must know what to do when faced with this hearing" (from clarksimsonmiller.com). If the response to a warning letter or a fine for a violation you did not commit is denied, you will want to request a hearing. In most associations, homeowners are entitled to notice and the opportunity to attend a fair hearing if disciplinary action is being considered or has been levied against them. Have your AI be especially complaisant when requesting a hearing regarding a matter that the board has contradicted you on.

> **Factoid:** *A.J. Vizzi spent almost $200,000 in legal fees to fight his HOA after it sued him for parking his pick-up truck in his own driveway. His pickup would not fit in the garage but the HOA was adamant he could not park in his own driveway. In the first go-round at court, Vizzi won—but the HOA, intractable, appealed. Vizzi prevailed again and the judge awarded him $187,000 to pay his lawyers. After reading about this case, I think there should be a Constitutional amendment that explicitly protects people's right to park in their own driveways.*

Best Practices for Requesting a Hearing

- Instruct your AI to draft a cordial letter expressing your commitment to HOA rules and requesting clarification on the violated covenant or policy.
- Ask for board assistance in resolving the issue, framing the request as a collaborative effort.
- Have your AI research the HOA's governing documents, local ordinances, and state/federal codes to support your case.
- Avoid accusations against neighbors or board members, maintaining a neighborly tone.
- Ask your AI to cite the specific bylaw or covenant granting your right to a hearing.

Prompt for Requesting a Hearing Before the Board

After your Master Prompt, add: "Draft a cordial letter to the secretary of [*association name, e.g., Happy Homes HOA*] in [*state, e.g., Wyoming*], addressing a violation notice and fine dated [date e.g., 4/4/2024] for *[issue, e.g., unapproved shingle color*]. Explain that my [date e.g., 4/24/2024] letter provided evidence of approval from the Architectural Committee, which the new chairperson denies, and request a hearing to present my case with evidence. Cite the bylaw granting my right to a hearing, keep the tone neighborly, and sign with 'Sincerely.'"

Best Practices for Prompting Your AI to Prepare a Defense for an HOA Disciplinary Hearing

- Instruct your AI to create a focused defense plan, citing prior approvals, bylaws, or state laws.
- Direct your AI to research best practices for HOA hearings (e.g., via https://clarksimsonmiller.com/hoa-disciplinary-hearing/) and relevant case studies.
- Gather evidence (e.g., stamped approvals, photos) and arguments against retroactive rule changes or unreasonable demands.
- Ask your AI to recommend additional strategies, such as requesting a waiver or mediation, to strengthen your case.
- Ensure your AI maintains a neighborly tone to preserve relationships with board members.

Research Prompt To Prepare a Defense in an HOA Disciplinary Hearing

After your Master Prompt, add: "Create a defense plan for my hearing with [association name, e.g., Oak HOA] in [state, e.g., New Jersey], regarding a violation notice and fine for unapproved shingle color, requiring removal at a cost of over $12,000. My [date] appeal letter included a stamped approval from the Architectural Committee, which the new chairperson denies. Research best practices for HOA hearings (e.g., https://clarksimsonmiller.com/hoa-disciplinary-hearing/) and relevant case studies. Argue that I have valid approval, retroactive rule changes are unfair, and the demand is unreasonable. Include evidence (e.g., stamped approval, shingle sample) and recommend strategies like requesting a waiver. Keep the tone neighborly and sign with 'Best regards.'"

IN CONCLUSION

This book equips homeowners with practical, AI-driven tools to navigate the complex landscape of HOA interactions, from requesting payoff statements and notifying boards about pets or service animals to addressing violations, filing complaints, and preparing for hearings. By leveraging AI to draft clear, professional communications and research governing documents or state resources, homeowners can assert their rights confidently while fostering cooperation with their boards. *HOA Warrior II* as a whole empowers you to take control of your HOA experience, transforming potential conflicts into opportunities for resolution. With AI as your ally, you can tackle bully boards, enforce fair treatment, and build stronger, more accountable communities—without losing your home or peace of mind.

Disclaimer: Shelly Marshall and Grok aren't attorneys. AI content is informational; verify with official sources (e.g., state sites like leg.state.fl.us for Florida or davis-stirling.com for California) and get legal advice for collections, foreclosures, or discrimination.

About the Author and her Choice to Write this Book

As a young hippie, I dreamed of saving the world with love, even placing daisies in the barrel of a cop's gun. But I quickly learned that good intentions alone couldn't change systemic injustices. Determined to make a difference, I earned a degree in Human Services and co-founded recovery centers, including the Hand of Hope halfway house for drug addicts in Denver and the Cortez Community Mission detox center for Native Americans in Colorado's Four Corners. In the 1970s, I helped develop one of the nation's first youth addiction treatment programs at St. Luke's Hospital in Denver. By the 1980s, I expanded my horizons, serving as a deputy sheriff in Bonner County, Idaho, driven by a relentless desire to help a troubled world.

My innate sense of fairness—my "Mama Grizzly" instinct—kicks in when I see people exploited. Writing self-help books has been my way of empowering myself and others, primarily through recovery literature for addicts and alcoholics, advocating for the verbally abused, and defending parents blamed for their children's struggles. But moving into a property owners' association (POA) was a wake-up call. When a director in my Grass Valley POA barked, "Shut up, we don't have to run every little thing by you people," I refused to stay silent. That moment sparked my journey into the murky world of planned development communities.

To fight for homeowner rights, I immersed myself in law and real estate, completing a California course with the Practicing Law Institute on limited-scope representation and attending workshops with the California Homeowner Law Institute. After eight years of battling for fairness in Grass Valley, winning some hard-fought victories, I grew disillusioned. New board members often fell into the same power traps as their predecessors. As Steve C., a fiercely independent lot owner in our community, aptly said, "In an association, you're only one election away from disaster.

"Despite the temptation to walk away, my drive to right wrongs persists. Laws favoring vendors, owners' inability to understand the high stakes of incorporated associations, and human nature's corruption when power is at play fueled HOA Warrior II. This book, born from the struggles of homeowners nationwide who've reached out since the first HOA Warrior, equips you with AI-driven tools to navigate HOA challenges. I'm now joining forces with advocates to reform or even outlaw oppressive HOA systems. If you're ready to fight for fairer communities, email info@HOAwarrior.com to join us. Together, we can be the change we seek, ensuring no homeowner suffers under privatized governance.

Made in the USA
Monee, IL
13 September 2026

62975573R10057